ANCIE
CEREM

A MAN OF THE SANDWICH ISLANDS IN A MASK.

ANCIENT RITES
AND
CEREMONIES

GRACE A. MURRAY

SENATE

Ancient Rites & Ceremonies

First published in 1929 by Alston Rivers Ltd, London.

This edition first published in 1996 by Senate, an imprint of
Random House UK Ltd, Random House, 20 Vauxhall Bridge
Road, London SW1V 2SA

ISBN 1 85958 158 7

Printed and bound in Guernsey by The Guernsey Press Co. Ltd

CONTENTS

CONTENTS

In Memory of my Best Friend

PREFACE

THE world is flooded with literature on every conceivable subject ; it would be, therefore, absurd to pretend that ancient customs had escaped this influx. Mere samples of various countries have been taken—a greater scope would have entailed a life's work.

To those who like probing beyond the surface, it will be interesting to note how the same customs are common to nations living thousands of miles apart, holding no intercourse with each other : among these Cannibalism may be quoted. Strabo even alludes, in about the year 600 B.C., to the inhabitants of England and Ireland as eaters of men ; while St. Jerome writes, that as a young man he saw a Scotsman eating human flesh, mentioning the most appetizing parts. These may be mere traditions—most people will prefer to believe they are.

Whether by sea or by land, from whichever direction peoples migrated, they would, more especially in very early times, bring their particular manners and customs with them. In the course of generations, the original and weaker country would be dominated by force of numbers. Indeed in primitive days, dominion was a universal plague, the Tartars being the most conspicuous example.

The worship of ancestors, who were raised to the dignity of gods, was one of the most dominant

PREFACE

features of ancient days ; to these they offered sacrifices for aid and protection. Among the chief factors in making people what they became, was shortage of food, and the rigour of an intensely cold climate. Whether, under the like conditions —the social fanatics, and mentally and morally unfit having predominated—we might ourselves, in course of time, return to these undesirable conditions—who knows ?

Apart from researches into the evidence of the most reliable travellers, voyagers, and navigators, the writer has had the privilege of first-hand information from those who have spent many years in such countries as the Congo, Fiji, Ceylon, and Poland. To these, and other friends, she is also indebted for the illustrations contained in this volume, and especially to Mrs. Harvey for her reproductions of old prints.

ANCIENT RITES AND CEREMONIES

ABYSSINIA

BEFORE Abyssinia was more intimately connected with that particular part of the world, it was loosely included in Ethiopia and Nubia, and associated with Arabs and Negroids. But after the discovery of Abyssinia by the Portuguese it seems to have been overlooked or forgotten for nearly 900 years, until about 1490. Their tradition asserts that they were descended from Shem, the son of Noah ; they also claim to be the only Christians in the world, yet Judaism and Mahometanism were woven into their rites and ceremonies.

The Abyssinian version of the Old Testament story was, that jealousy, the prevailing root of all evil, descended with other sins from our first parents. Adam and Eve had enjoyed a period of enchanted rapture in Paradise ; one evening when Adam had gone to heaven for his daily visit to pray, the Devil looked in to see Eve ; and after making a few personal remarks of a flattering nature, enquired after her spouse. Eve replied by informing him of the whereabouts of her husband at which the Devil smiled doubtingly ; but no word escaped his lips, in spite of Eve's enquiring as to the reason of his mysterious smile. Eventually, with much apparent reluctance, the Devil broke it very gently that Eve was a deceived wife. " How can this be ? " replied the lady contemptuously, " for I know there is no woman created except myself ! " The Devil commiserated with her sadly on her simplicity ; at the same time

asking, whether she would credit his words were she
shown another woman ; and upon Eve's assenting
—he held up a mirror.

Father Jerome Lobo, the Jesuit, sent to Abyssinia by King John II of Portugal in 1490, testified
to the existence of the unicorn, but as no one ever
seems to have seen it properly, one feels justified in
being a trifle sceptical. We also hear how the
Abyssinians "eat flesh raw, and, they have a
method of obtaining it which seems hardly credible,
but is a fact." One of these methods is given by
Dr. Bruce, in 1791, when he met some travellers
who were driving a cow, and presently discovered,
that the wound caused by a "steak," cut from the
hind quarters of the animal, was then closed in by
drawing the skin over it, and the application of
some clay. The animal was afterwards driven on
until there was demand for another meal.

At their feast called *Brind*, lumps of flesh were
cut out of a bull or cow ; the roaring of the poor
beast being the signal for the commencement of
the feast. Before serving their masters with food
and drink, the servants always previously tasted it.
And, as in Abyssinia there was nothing considered
so disgusting as licking the fingers after eating, a
piece of bread was provided for wiping their
mouths. Indeed, in some respects, the manners
of these people, although the reasons might not
always be intelligible to us, were beyond reproach ;
for example, when persons of importance sneezed,
everyone within reach immediately exclaimed,
" God forgive you, master."

In the higher classes, marriage took place about
Christmas, or after Ascension Day. After which,
husband and wife kept separate tables ; or, if they
were of the same opinion, each supplied his own
previously prepared food. It was esteemed unlaw-

ful to have more than one wife at a time, but they were allowed to live with a number of wives, as polygamy was not considered detrimental to society. Divorce was not uncommon, the main causes being—the want of children, or bodily infirmity on either side ; infidelity was usually arranged by compromise.

If a married couple were unable to agree, the children were divided, the decision being made by the priest : usually, the father took the eldest boy, and the mother the eldest girl. Should any complications arise after this distribution, the matter was settled by the casting of votes. At an earlier period, marriage was never performed in churches, nor had a priest any part in the matter : a man might take as many wives as he chose, should he not consider it prudent to restrict himself to one, a misgiving which, apparently, often beset these Abyssinians. If it, however, happened that a couple felt satisfied with each other, they went before " a court of the elders of the town " to arrange that any property of which they might be possessed should be joined together for the benefit of both ; neither having the power to dispose of it, without the consent of the other.

No Abyssinian was jealous of a man with whom he was on terms of friendship, whatever familiarities might have taken place between him and his wife ; otherwise an erring wife would usually be deprived of her fortune and be turned out of the house, a week only being allowed for her to find a living.

At *Amhàra* and *Tigrè*, when a man considered his daughter old enough for marriage, he exhibited her at the door, under the pretence of spinning or cleaning corn : at the same time she was instructed how " to turn up the whites of her eyes, when men or strangers pass, and put on a look between bravery and modesty when replying to questions." The children were soon sold, the price being a cotton shirt, or a piece of cloth. Should the man be content with his purchase, he sent a piece of white cloth, dipped in the blood of a fowl, round to her friends. He could rid himself of her when he chose; and at the expiration of any time previously arranged, she, also, was free to quit him.

There was a revolting practice that when a woman lost one or more children she would, in hopes of saving one lately born, cut off a piece from her left ear, roll it in a slice of bread, and swallow it. Others shaved one side of their head until the child was fully grown.

It was considered improper for women to wash or sew any article of clothing, these duties being more suitable to men : indeed, in certain districts, it was even thought a disgrace for women to milk cows or goats. Among other prejudices, might be mentioned the Abyssinians' aversion to hares, of which there were a great number : anyone touching these animals was regarded as polluted.

Among their omens was whether the notes of certain birds were heard on the right or left side. Important undertakings, such as war, or a hunting expedition with every probability of success, would be suddenly abandoned merely because the chirp of a small bird was heard on the left side : which was the propitious side for the return journey but the wrong side for setting out. At *Tigrè*, the black and white falcons were particularly associated with omens : should they fly away on the approach of a traveller it indicated disaster ; should they, however, remain perched on the trees looking at him, all would be well. An animal which had been killed by a lion or a leopard, was usually considered good eating, owing to these beasts being regarded as Christian : very different was it, had they been killed by that "disgusting scavenger," a hyena, which was regarded as part of the Mussulman religion and, consequently, unfit for food.

These people were great believers in a species of malevolent spirits called *Bouda* ; according to Mansfield Parkyns, the trade of blacksmith, which was hereditary, was regarded with more or less opprobrium ; for with few exceptions they were believed to be sorcerers, possessing the power of turning into hyenas and other animals. One of the customs of the Abyssinians was to conceal a child's baptismal name, which was usually the name of some saint, and call it by some nickname given it by their mothers on leaving the church : the reason being, that the *Bouda* could not in any way injure one whose name he did not know. Otherwise, he took a special kind of straw, and having muttered some incoherent words over it, bent it into a circle, then hid it under a stone. At the moment the straw was being bent, the person would be taken ill ; and should it snap while this was being done, the person would certainly die.

In certain localities, should the husband on his return from work, leaving his wife at home, find that a spear had been stood at the door of his hut, he would go away, knowing that some other man was with her. After allowing sufficient time to elapse for the visitor's departure, whether it was a neighbour, brother, or some stranger, his wife was closely questioned. Supposing the visitor to have been a stranger, no offence would be taken ; she would, however, be asked if she had made a good bargain, in which case she was commended. Should, on the contrary, the bargain have been a poor one, she would be rebuked—this being the custom of the country.

ANCIENT NATIONS OF CENTRAL AMERICA

AZTECS OF MEXICO, MAYAS OF YUCATAN, CUBA, ETC.

THE existence of these nations became known in Europe, only at the beginning of the 16th century. They comprised cities of many-storied stone buildings, vast temples, densely populated, and in a remarkably high state of civilization. Ruled by kings and nobles each with heraldic arms, divided into a number of states, with governors and retinues, and an extremely superior order of intelligence especially devoted to mathematics and astronomy, with every virtue and balanced mentality of law and order. Yet these people were saturated with a form of religion, the wooden and clay idols of which demanded a constant supply of human blood to appease their wrath, or for the conferring of their benefits.

To have arrived at the state of civilization which they had reached, must have involved a vast number of centuries of gradual development; there is unfortunately no translatable record which gives us any clue to their earlier history, except that perhaps it originated in the North American continent. All that can be said is, there were found, in about the year 1500 A.D., two nations, the Aztecs and Mayas, who had passed the zenith of civilization—the how and whence is unknown; and that principally owing to constant warfare, probably combined with over-population, the fighting men being so reduced that the first strangers from Spain conquered and annexed the falling Empire of the Aztecs, while the Mayas were exterminated in their own wars. The construction and development of many centuries, and its establishment of probably 4000 years were thus swept away by their conquest in about 1523. These people are known as Ancient Mexicans.

There appears to have existed many tribes of the same nation, of the same origin, who were mound dwellers ; mounds of remarkable workmanship occupied many miles in area. Another group, at a different place, were cavern dwellers, living in caves, in almost inaccessible positions ; these also extended over a very large area, which resulted in a constant state of civil war between communities and tribes, and accounted for their disruption and eventual conquest.

All these people lived in a state of communism and socialism, under the supreme head of the confederation whose palace was in the town of Mexico. Every man was obliged to marry at the age of twenty : failing this he was deemed only fit to be a slave.

Any man or woman disguised as the other sex was killed ; while the privilege of being drunk was reserved for men over seventy.

Names were not transmitted from father to son, and children belonged to the community.

There was said to be a period of 104 years before the descendants of the first man and the first woman settled at Aztlam : the *Chichimecas* were one of these earliest tribes. While migrating for eighty years in obedience to the voice of their gods, they stopped at various places, leaving behind a number of their people, until they had occupied North, South, East and West of the Lake of Mexico.

The first of the exodus to arrive at the lake were

the *Su-chimilei* : they were gardeners, and established a community of that name on the South side. Thus all sides of the lake were occupied. When a fifth group arrived, finding all the territory in possession, they marched away to the mountains, and founded the town of *Quahuac*—signifying Eagle. There was yet a sixth group, who settled still further to the East ; these people aided the Spaniards in their conquest of Mexico.

All these groups lived harmoniously with one another, and established laws for the government of the race. Three hundred years later arrived people, under the leadership of a man called Mexi. During their exodus they stopped for periods and peopled certain districts, according to the command of their god *Vitzilipuztli*, to whom they offered human sacrifices.

These people founded a number of settlements and finally arrived at *Chapultepec*, conquering all the previous settlers. Their god, Vitzilipuztli, appeared in a vision to the people's priest, and commanded them to establish themselves at that part of the lake where they would find an eagle perched on a cactus, the root of which was in a rock ; this the priest found after a short search : the eagle with spread wings was looking at the sun, holding a small bird in its talons. At this spot they built their town, which they called *Tenochillan*. Hence, the Mexican coat-of-arms is an eagle gazing at the sun, with outspread wings, holding a serpent—emblem of fertility—in its claws, with one foot on a cactus branch. When the houses were erected, the Mexicans raised a temple to their god. These people, both men and women, were big and tawny coloured ; their hairless faces broad, their noses flat : they were a long-lived people.

Friar Marcus de Nica in 1539, speaking of the *Chichimecas*, says that they were looked upon by other tribes in the light of saints and priests. They lived in the woods, and "they eate such things as they of the country give them of almes." Certain of their small temples had small round window spaces, full of dead men's skulls. In front of the temple was a great round ditch for the purpose of immolation. From time to time "they of this valley cast lots whose lucke (honour) it shal be to be sacrificed, and they make him great cheere, on whom the lotte falleth, and with great joy they crowne him with flowres upon a bed prepared in the sayd ditch all full of flowres and sweete hearbes, on which they lay him along, and lay great store of dry wood on both sides of him, and set it on fire on eyther part, and so he dyeth." By which it appears that the victim "tooke great pleasure" in being sacrificed. He was afterwards beatified, and worshipped for that year; at the end of which period, his head was set up, with others, "within those windows." On the other hand, prisoners were burnt in another ditch, without flowers or any ceremonies, merely as a sacrifice—to whom, it is not stated.

Ancient records were expressed in hieroglyphics —a cycle of time was 52 solar years; this again was subdivided into four periods—each of 13 years: this number of 13 was a key to their divisions of time. A month was 20 days; the year, consisting of 18 months, counted in thirteens. By this arrangement, given the name of the day and its corresponding number, the name of the month was obvious. There were no weeks of seven days. In some places, the 3rd, 8th, 13th, and 18th were days of rest. At the end of each year, five days were intercalated.

In certain districts water was worshipped, for as
they said, water caused their crops to grow, and
thus maintained their life ; also, their ancestors
did so.

Near *Cicuic* we are told that the natives " chawe
their meate but little, and raven up much, and
holding the flesh with their teeth, they cut it with
rasors of stone." Lopez de Somara in 1540 gives
a quaint description of their buffaloes, which were
their staple article of food, large herds roaming all
over the plains : " They have a great bunch upon
their fore shoulders, and more haire on their fore
part than on their hinder part : and it is like wooll.
They have as it were an horse-mane upon their
backe bone, and much haire and very long from
the knees downeward. They have great tuffes of
haire hanging downe their foreheads, and it
seemeth that they have beardes, because of the
great store of haire hanging downe at their chinnes
and throates." At *Cevola,* the Mexicans had very
beautiful turquoises, which they exchanged for
" oxe-hydes " ; the women wore rich girdles of
turquoises, with the same fine jewels hanging from
their nostrils and ears ; they also wore double or
treble collars made of the same jewel.

At *Colima,* as in various other places, the
Indians painted as well as tattooed their faces ;
many of them also wore shells and bones in their
ears ; with a girdle of various colours round their
waist, in the centre of which, at the back, was a
round bunch of feathers, which " hangeth downe
behind like a tayle." Furthermore we are told,
" This is a mightie people, well feitured, and
without any grossenesse."

After battle, the Indians took out the heart of
some of their enemies, and ate it ; others they
burned. Fernando Alarchon says he saw one

woman "which ware a garment like a little Mantle, which clad her from the waste downe to the ground, of a Deeres skin well dressed."

Like the ancient Peruvians, many of the chiefs believed that they were the children of the Sun. It is difficult to understand how some of the Spanish missionaries declared with the greatest assurance that they also were children of the Sun.

Human sacrifices to the god Quetzaaletatl was a gruesome ceremony. For forty days before that event, a slave, who must be perfectly sound and without blemish, wore the garments of the idol to resemble it. Nine days before the sacrifice, the man was warned of his death ; if he showed signs of fear, they bled him, and made him drink his blood, mixed in cocoa. At midnight on the day of the sacrifice, the martyr was slain, and his heart was offered up first to the moon, and then to the god. The body was later thrown from the top of the steps of the Temple and seized by some of the people, who made a meal of it next day.

Other sacrifices there were of unimaginable details : sometimes they would dress a man in the clothes of a god and march him through the streets, to be adored as if he were actually a live god. In some years as many as 20,000 prisoners were thus sacrificed ; each particular part—tongue, nose, fingers—was separately sacrificed, and solemnly offered to the gods.

The Indians were evidently remarkably circum-spect in regard to their marriages. If a man had a daughter of marriageable age, he went to some district, and asked if there was any man who desired to wed her. In which case, the father of the young man brought the bride-elect some offering. After that the marriage was considered final ; the company danced and sang ; and when

night came " the parents tooke them, and left
them together in a place where no body might see
them." It was not usual for " maydes " to converse with men before their marriage ; instead of
this dallying they busied themselves at home. And
should any " have company " with other men before their marriage, their outraged husbands for-
sook them, and went into other countries, while
they " were accompted naughty packs."

The climate of these people was hardly ideal, for
we hear " they use every morning to drive thorow
the towne (Vera Cruz) above two thousand head of
cattell, to take away the ill vapours of the earth."

In the wildest western regions of Mexico, John
Chiltern says, " their common armour is bowes and
arrowes (flintheaded) ; they use to eate up such
Christians as they came by." He thanked God
that because he was " leane " and the Indians
thought he was diseased, they escorted him away
from their territory. It appears, also, that the
Indians " take a great pride in killing a Christian,
and to weare any part of him where he hath any
haire growing, hanging it about their necks, and
so are accounted for valiant men."

In some provinces of Mexico, cocoa grows
abundantly, " the Indians make drinke of it, and
in like manner meat to eat. It goeth currantly (in
the form of beans) for money in any market or
faire." Intoxicants appealed greatly to these
people. " They are soone drunke, and given to
much beastlinesse " ; they hankered especially
after the native wine called *pulque*, a fermented
drink made from the honey of the flower of a form
of cactus, which had an odour of putrid meat, to
which were added some roots and herbs.

The paper upon which the Aztecs wrote their
hieroglyphics was made of the fibre of this plant ;

the prickles at the edge of the leaves served for
pins and nails.

By nature they were a simple folk, timid and
cowardly : " They use divers times to talke with
the divell, to whom they do certine sacrifices and
oblations." They also sacrificed to a stone,
erected on a mound, named *Cowa ;* on special days
old men and young children were sacrificed to this
image.

The *Chichimecas* wore their hair down to the
knees, and " doe also colour their faces greene,
yellow, red, and blew, which maketh them to
seeme very ougly and terrible to behold."

The king's palace contained more than three
hundred rooms, with three principal entrances—
one facing West towards the lake, another East
towards the mountains, the third opening to the
South. On stated days a preacher declaimed to
the king and his assembled court against the errors
of their ways. In front of the principal temple
was placed the stone on which prisoners of war
were sacrificed ; over four hundred priests were
attached to this temple. Another temple was
dedicated to the God of Air.

Some of their laws were most drastic : treason
was punished by cutting off the legs and arms, and
all the culprit's children became slaves unto the
fifth generation. In some cases of infidelity the
man was burnt alive, and during the process he
was sprinkled with water and salt ; the woman
met with rather a less barbarous fate, for she was
hanged. For theft, the culprit became the slave
of the owner of the property. If the son of a noble
dissipated his heritage, he was strangled. A man
found drunk had his head publicly shaved, in
addition to which his house was destroyed ; on the
second occasion of his inebriety he was killed.

Among the various laws, no man was permitted to build a house without the permission of the king. If a nobleman made his escape from the enemy and returned to his own town, he was put to death ; but if a plebeian did the same thing, he was recompensed.

There was a kind of League of Nations arrangement, when messengers were sent to the old people of both sexes of the offending state, warning them of the awful consequences of war, and asking them to prevail on the authorities to remain at peace. Twenty days were given to make up their minds for second thoughts ; after another twenty days' grace, war was declared.

In the year 1450, owing to a cold wave passing over the country, followed by years of pestilence and famine, it was decided to offer up sacrifices of human bodies in a wholesale manner, to appease the gods and to change the tide of events. The three rulers of the empire resolved on a state of war between the three states. Equal numbers of men on each side agreed to fight for a few days, at the beginning of each month : it was a triangular combat lasting for years, by which each side in turn supplied a number of killed as prisoners to be sacrificed. This answered various purposes : it indirectly eliminated the unfit, thereby giving the fit a better chance to live ; the gods were also appeased every eighteen months (their solar year) at their annual festival.

Meanwhile, in 1462, King *Netzahualcoyotzin* left at his death sixty sons and fifty daughters. He was known as the wisest, noblest, and most powerful king who had ever ruled, and specially learned in physiology. According to him all the idols that were worshipped were false gods, demon enemies of the human race. He recognized the evidence of

God in the Sun and Earth : the Earth, his mother, was begotten by the Sun, his father. This king abolished the sacrifice of the people's kith and kin, though prisoners and slaves might be used for that purpose, in accordance with ancient customs.

Human life was held in little account, for in 1486 at the inauguration of their principal temple to *Huitzilopochtl*, the principal idol of the nation, the whole of their prisoners and captives were mustered from all the states of the Empire ; the estimated number of these was 80,000. All these were sacrificed, and their heads were collected and deposited in niches in the Temple, specially built to hold them. Besides these, another 20,000 slaves and prisoners of former wars were added to the sacrifice, making a total of about 100,000.

This supreme god " was represented under a human shape, sitting on a throne supported by an azure globe (hemisphere), which they call'd heaven. Four poles or sticks came out from two sides of this globe, at the ends of which serpents heads were carved ; the whole making a litter which the priests carried on their shoulders whenever the idol was shown in public." There were a variety of divinities : besides others were the heart of the Heavens—a mixture of thunder, lightning, and tempest.

Each state of existence was a dream : the present life a dream which would be realized at the awakening by death.

It was the priests who excited the people in the name of their gods, who demanded human flesh. The eating of the enemy was part of a soldier's education to enable him to lay aside all feelings of humanity, to excite his ferocity and accustom him to the horrors of carnage, and which, moreover, was the path of his religion.

In 1500 the astrologers predicted that a new
Nation would establish itself in Mexico : these
new people, the *Toltecs*, were the descendants of
a previous king, and would come from the East.
At this time the king's son, a prodigy and an inhuman atrocity, at the age of three pushed his
nurse into a well, because he had seen her in company with a man of the Court. At the age of
seven, he had four of his counsellors strangled
because he loved slaughter. One king, who died
in 1515, left 145 sons, of whom 14 were legitimate.

The punishment of infidelity was strangling,
and it was so rigidly carried out that even a king
on discovering some time after the event that a
concubine was married and had children, immediately caused her to be strangled for her deception.
Long names were composed of two or three words :
such as *Mtecuhzoma*—severe ruler. Kings and
great men were buried in caves : legend attributed
the caves, or bowels of the Earth, to be the place
whence the ancestors of the race emerged ; and
it was near these caves that the high priest, or
great Prophet lived, who was regarded as being in
close relation with the gods, and whose commands
the king obeyed.

The idols were housed in a chapel. On the
occasions of great festivals, the high priest, known
as the " Great Seer," made obeisance to the gods,
conversed with them in an ecstatic state, making
hideous grimaces and writhings ; when he emerged
from the " diabolical trance," he told those around
what the spirits had imparted to him. Human
sacrifices were held at the same time, and the high
priest would hold the bleeding heart of the victim
against the wooden idol's mouth. In an underground dungeon of this temple, lay the bodies of

the great lord chieftains who had fallen in battle ;
be the distance what it might, the bodies of these
chiefs had to be brought to their burial home.   So
great was the belief in the happiness of a future
life, that many who were oppressed by disease or
hardship, begged the high priest to accept them
as living sacrifices, and allow them to enter the
portal to the underground passages, and roam
about in the abyss of darkness until starved to
death.   It is said that this underground catacomb
extended more than " thirty leagues underground."

The priests never married, and when children,
were deprived of their virility.   At certain festivals
when they were constrained to be intoxicated, the
king brought to them the unmarried daughters of
the chieftains ; and if one of these showed later,
signs of becoming a mother and in course of time
a son was born, he could be brought up as the
priest's successor.

It was not customary to sleep on bedsteads,
however noble a lord might be ; instead, they
slept on braided mats and the soft skins of animals,
and were covered with the most delicate fabrics.
Their food consisted of meat killed in hunting :
rabbits, deer, armadillos, etc. ; their bread was
made from maize ; they drank a mixture of
chocolate, water, and pounded maize. Their
intoxicating drink was *pulque ;* this was consumed with crushed fruits.

The Rain-god existed in four reservoirs ; in
other words, it flowed from four directions.   From
the East, the water was exceeding good, and the
rain from it came at the time of growing crops.
From the West, part of the water was unwanted ;
it produced a fungus which rotted the crops,
bringing death and famine. From the third

quarter, the North, the rain turned to ice or caused floods. In the fourth quarter, the South, the rain induced growth, but the crops soon scorched up from heat. It was said that this Rain-god, in its efforts to produce rain, created many ill-fated weaklings in the form of dwarfs, who lived in the four reservoirs and carried sticks in their hands ; also jars, into which they poured water from the huge casks, from which they poured out water as they were commanded. Children were, in the first or sixth month of the year, sacrificed to the "god of rain, tempest, and mountains." This sacrifice was called—paying their debts to these gods.

There was also a ritual for confessions to be made to the Earth-god (" God of Space ") ; the idea prevailed that by this confession the sinner was purged from his sins, and could no longer be reached by the secular law. The symbol of these particular sins, which they laid at the feet of the god, consisted of knotting together two slender threads made of dry maize husks. These knotted threads were laid on a dish of braided grass ; while in a long speech they begged for forgiveness. The priest then gave the supplicant some sort of penance to perform, told them they were pardoned, and could sin anew.

As far as can be gathered, for out of superstition the Spaniards destroyed nearly all the ancient records, 104 years later, two cycles of years—the *Toltecs*, who were at that period the dominant people, on leaving their country became wanderers, until they settled and founded the city of *Toluca* in 543 of our epoch. They built palaces of stone in which their history was engraved ; in the temple stood the Frog goddess of water, fashioned out of a single emerald. These people inhabited more than a thousand miles of land, with magnificent cities and temples ; the ruins of all these were still standing up to the time of the Spanish conquest.

Their kings were represented as being of pale colour, and bearded as were the Spaniards : in fact, the first Spaniards led by Cortez, were mistaken for returning Toltecs : these people were eventually conquered by the Aztecs. In about 959 A.D. civil war broke out, and during the three years of fighting which ensued, it was estimated that over three million Toltecs perished, with over two million of their opponents ; and the country was laid waste. Shortly afterwards there was a famine, followed by twenty-four years of drought, and these people became practically extinct. The *Chichimecas*, from the North, took possession of this country ; it is said that the source of these people was Tartary. They claimed the Sun as their father, and the Moon as their mother : these were their only gods. The outline which we call the " Man in the Moon " was recognized by the Mexicans as a rabbit, which was made in it by the Sun, from the Earth in which it was generated. As was the case of the ancient Egyptians, the Moon (Isis) was the astral, under the symbol of a woman. A drunken man, irresponsible for his actions, was said to have a rabbit in him. The god of drunkenness was also named " rabbit " (which seems distinctly disrespectful to the Moon). To illustrate the numerous degrees and condition of the inebriated, there were 400 *pulque* gods ; all of these wore a crescent-shaped ornament representing the rabbit in the Moon, and were related to the Earth-goddess—the goddess of sin and temptation. These gods were associated with the floral fêtes and festivities, as well as with the Bacchanalian orgies at harvesting time. When a man died from excess of alcohol, the others made a feast of him.

Out of their knowledge of astronomy, the Mexicans estimated the true direction of the four cardinal points, from the position of the stars on certain dates. Venus was their principal star, from which they made many calculations; this planet they called "the Lord of the Dawn," either when a morning star or evening star. Sacrifices of prisoners were offered to it, for what object is not stated. The Snail was the symbol of birth.

Men's dress consisted of a girdle, the width of a man's hand, bound several times round their loins, one end hanging down in front, the other behind. Over this, large mantles or capes with a hole were fastened on the shoulders; on their feet were sandals of hemp, or tanned deerskin. When going to war, the warriors wore tiger and bear skins. Women wore a skirt from the waist down, and a sack-like jacket reaching to the hips. They also wore leg and wrist ornaments of feather work, as well as arm-rings, bead necklaces, and ear-rings.

Bishop Landa says in describing these people : "They wore their hair long, like women ; on the top they burnt a sort of large tonsure ; they let the hair grow round it, while the hair of the tonsure remained short. They bound the hair in braids about the head with the exception of one lock, which they allowed to hang down behind like a tassel." "The priests of Yucatan," observes Bancroft, "wore their hair long, uncombed, and often saturated with sacrificial blood." There was no complexity in the arrangement of women's hair ; it was arranged in long strands, which fell partly over the breast and partly over the back.

To raise the right arm over the left breast, with the hand over the left shoulder, was a sign of submission and of peaceful intent. The North American Indians expressed the same idea by holding out the right hand, palm upward ; some raised their hands empty-handed, or clasped their hands together.

Montezuma, the last king of the Aztecs, was a magnificent royalty ; he was carried about on the shoulders of his nobles, supporting a platform richly ornamented with gold, feathers, and flowers. He never wore his clothes more than once, and never ate or drank out of the same vessel twice. He kept all kinds of birds, fish, and animals ; those specimens he was unable to obtain he commanded to be fashioned of gold and silver.

Montezuma (spelt in different ways) was on the throne of Mexico when the Spaniards began their conquest ; believing they were the descendants of the true owners of the land (Toltecs), he surrendered his country to them, and died a prisoner.

CELEBES

In *Celebes* the native houses were built on posts, reached by a ladder which could be pulled up, to prevent the entrance of dogs; for a dog was considered an unclean animal, and if by any mischance one touched a human body, he or she would be obliged to wash away the contamination in the nearest river. The market was open for an hour before sunrise, and at the same hour before sunset. It would have been inexcusable for a man to be seen in the market; he would have been subjected to the greatest insults from the youths and maidens; a man's occupation was supposed to be of a much more serious nature than bargaining for eatables.

The relatively longish nose of a European was quite in opposition to their standard of beauty, where a flat broad nose was *chic*. So, almost as soon as they were born, at each meal, infants' noses were carefully softened by oil and warm water, and pressed flat. At the age of five or six, all male children were removed from their mothers, and placed under the charge of a friend or relation, lest they grew up spoilt or effeminate. At the age of fifteen or sixteen they were returned to their parents, that age being the legal one for marriage.

From childhood and all through their lives, their finger-nails were stained red. It was also the custom to stain their teeth either green or red, using the citron for that purpose. Some, in their desire to out-rival others, even had their front teeth pulled out, and had gold or silver ones substituted. The men, universally, were even more decorated than the women, with jewellery and precious stones.

The Sagas of old had instructed these people that the heavens never had a beginning. The Sun and Moon always exercised their power, and these two had existed without jealousy; until, owing to some quarrel as to who should be the mightier, the Sun began chasing the Moon to punish her; during this chase the Moon was delivered of Earth.

From this beginning, a primitive mythology was given to account for the gods of the Sea, as well as for the tempests, and subterranean gods who were responsible for minerals, and for earthquakes and their awful destruction. The Moon was kept continually busy in giving birth to new parts of the Earth, and renewing those which had been scorched up by the heat of the Sun. Finally, it was believed that the Sun and Moon had become reconciled, each recognizing their relative duties to Earth, on the understanding that they would divide between them the Empire of Heaven: the Sun reigning for one half of the twenty-four hours—the day; the Moon the other twelve hours —the night. If these people were slightly out in their reckoning, what matter? No one can deny that the theory was an ingenious one.

In doubt as to which religion to adopt, whether Christian or Mahometan, the king of Celebes was advised to adopt the one which arrived first in his country, for it was said: God would never permit a wrong to arrive before a right, if both were on their way together. It is related that the Mahometans arrived first; so, Mahometans they became, that religion being acknowledged as the standard religion of their country.

According to Wallace's own experiences in 1853 in the interior of the country, scarcely any native had seen a white man before; the result being that wherever he went dogs barked, children screamed, women ran away, and men stared; even the pack-horses along the roads when they caught sight of him, started aside and bolted into the jungle, while the ugly little buffaloes stretched out their necks, stared, then rushed away as if pursued by some demon.

The burning mountain, the torrent, and the lake were the abodes of their deities; also, certain trees and birds were supposed to exercise special influence on their actions and destiny. Wild and exciting festivals were held to propitiate their deities or demons. Villages, not more than three or four miles apart, had languages of their own, unintelligible to all the others.

A Religious Fanatic (Ceylon).

Facing page 35

CEYLON

At one time the Portuguese possessed part of the coast, from which they made frequent incursions into the capital (Candy), on several occasions burning it down. The king of Ceylon eventually, to secure peace, paid them a yearly tribute of three elephants : the Dutch, from Batavia, also came to their assistance, and finally the Portuguese were driven out ; the price of their assistance was the installation of the Dutch into the land vacated, for they seized Colombo, as well as other places along the coast.

The earliest inhabitants were called *Wadas ;* they were primitive nomads, hill men, who neither planted nor tilled the soil, subsisting entirely on wild plants, and the prey they trapped ; they had neither houses nor shelter, but lived and slept in the open. In appearance, Pyrard, in 1601, tells us that they resembled the African negro.

At a later date the inhabitants more nearly resembled Europeans, and it has been suggested that they originated from China ; they were wholly lacking in the barbaric element, both sexes being decently clothed. Their laws on caste were strict ; but certain trades, such as carpenters, painters or tool-sharpeners, had, within certain limits, the same standing as the nobility, although they might not eat with them, nor marry into their ranks. Nor would anyone eat with a barber, and men of this caste were not allowed to be seated.

Potters were a class still more inferior ; they wore no " camisoles " (a sort of gown) ; they must neither be seated nor eat with other men ; but they might pour water into their mouths from the same drinking vessel as a man of higher caste, so long as they did not touch it with their lips. Men who washed clothes were a numerous class, but their patrons were expected to be of the élite. Weavers ranked beneath the launderers. There were also soothsayers, astrologers, foretellers of events, and of good or bad days, of the date of birth and sex of children, of success or failure of undertakings ; they predicted, in fact, everything relating to the future. It was they who beat the drums, danced in the temples, were p resent at the sacrifices, consumed all the offerings to the gods.

Basket-makers were of a still lower grade, as were elephant keepers. Each married into their respective castes, and the same profession passed from father to son for generations. The lowest of all grades being the paid soldiers ; they were, in fact, considered vile, because they were slaves and outcastes from father to son ; they were not even permitted to be served by other slaves. Knox speaks also of a " degraded " class : vagabonds, pedlars, gypsies, and miraculous conjurors all in one ; these sycophants with their abject mannerisms were nomads and wanderers, and were reputed to be inconceivably incestuous. One of the king's punishments was to exile a lawbreaker into the hands of these vagabonds, and this was looked upon as something worse than death.

The Cingalese worshipped several gods ; their principal divinity being *Offa Palla Maups*, that is, Creator of Heaven and Earth. Other gods were subordinate to him, and also included the souls who had lived an exemplary life on earth. Another of their highest divinities was called *Buddou*, whose special duty seems to have been the protection of souls ; he, having at one time descended to Earth, occasionally made himself visible under a tree called *Bogaha*. From the summit of a high mountain he rose to heaven where the imprint of one of his feet is still said to be visible. The Sun, called *Irri*, was, too, an object of worship, as was also the Moon, called *Hauda*.

There were some very ancient pagodas, possibly erected more than a thousand years ago, but all records of the builders are lost; these show evidence of an earlier and more energetic race.

The Cingalese had three classes of priests: the first and highest class, who wore yellow cassocks, belonged to the order of *Buddou*; their principal temple was at *Digligi*; they possessed an immense revenue, and were a great power and authority in the land. According to their rule, they ate meat only once a day, but they must not be aware that any animal had been killed for this purpose. The second order of priests were called *Koppuh*; they seem to have more resembled lay priests; their principal duty was to present rice and other offerings to the gods (idols); otherwise they apparently lived in much the same manner as ordinary folk.

The third order was known by the name of *Jaddeses*; their little temples were profusely painted with swords, armour, and various images. These priests offered sacrifices to propitiate demon spirits in order that they should render assistance in the curing of disease; although the people did not actually worship these evil spirits, they had a great respect for their power, and frequently sacrificed cockerels in order to obtain their protection.

Knox says: " I have seen men and women, so agitated by some supernatural cause, that they seemed as 'possessed.' In this state some ran shouting into the woods as if demented; some merely sat and trembled from head to foot, with facial contortions and speaking incoherently—

some died. I can state that frequently I have heard the devil bay in the night, like a dog. This has always been the signal, that the king has ordered the death of a subject. The reasons given that it is the cry of the devil are these : (1) There is no other sound from any living thing that resembles it ; (2) The sound transfers itself from place to place, quicker than the flight of any bird ; (3) Even dogs tremble at the sound ; and also, it is common knowledge that it is so."

Though without any form of clock or time-piece, these people divided the day between sunrise and sunset into thirty parts, partly by guesswork and guided partly by one particular flower, which opened regularly about seven hours before sunset.

All exchanges were made by barter ; every man working for himself, but never for another.

These people had a strange habit of humiliating themselves towards others : instead of saying, " I have made," they would observe " this un-worthy dog has made." If asked as to the num-ber of their children, the reply would be— of so many dogs, male and female.

Marriage was merely a matter of convenience ; if unsuited to one another, they separated in the same easy fashion : any complication in the way of the children was easily adjusted, boys remain-ing with their father, and girls with their mother. It was quite common for men and women to have four or five " trial " marriages, before a final adjustment ; but it was rare that a man had more than one wife, though it frequently occurred that a woman had two husbands.

Some of the marriage customs resembled those of the Tartar tribes : when a man desired to marry, he first went to the house of his mistress to purchase her clothes. If the sum offered was

A Group of Cingalese: Grandfather, Father and Family.

Facing page 38

a sufficiently good one, a proof that he was in easy circumstances, she was perfectly willing to sell them. The same evening he brought them back to her, and he did not leave his prospective bride until the following morning. By that time they had settled the day for their marriage, which took place at the bride's home ; at this ceremony they ate out of the same dish, and their thumbs were tied together.

Custom permitted brothers to share one wife. The Cingalese not being of a jealous disposition, so long as a woman favoured a man of equal social standing as her husband, no one troubled. Men always treated women with the greatest respect, the utmost licence being given them. There was, however, one stringent law ; no woman was permitted to squat in the presence of a man.

In most ways they were a simple, happy people : all day they sang ; and if awakened at night, they sang away the hours until the morning dawned. They never ate meat ; a little rice, with the juice of a lemon to drink, satisfied their needs.

But among their kings, the lust of cruelty was strong ; they were autocrats, with unlimited power to carry out their acts of cruelty and brutality ; in order to make a man confess a crime, or give the name of his confederates, they would torture him to death by pulling out his nails, burning with hot irons, and other revolting practices ; sometimes elephants were used to mutilate and crush a prisoner to death. Eventually, his or her body would be thrown to the dogs, who, usually scenting a feast, followed in the wake of the procession of people.

Among the higher ranks of the Cingalese they had their dead cremated ; but in the lower castes they were buried in the forest.

CONGO

CONGO, situated on the west side of Equatorial Africa, is called after the great river of that name : it covers a large area, roughly speaking about the size of France and Spain, and includes the districts of Loango, Congo proper, Angola, and Benguela. In this part of the world Pigmies, or *Matimbas*, were first seen.

At *Gobbi*, the capital of *Loango*, an inhabitant who was paying a visit to a friend, would, before other matters had been discussed, be first offered one of his host's wives ; at all times moral laxness on the part of a woman received more eulogy than reproach ; yet the empire of man was absolute, and every woman was contented in proportion to the brutality of her man. Women sat apart while men ate, submission to that sex being so complete that were she spoken to she went on her knees. Two or three children were usually the limit of their family.

According to Merolla, the missionary, when a stranger visited their huts, the women were obliged to surrender themselves to the guest for the two following nights. A Capucin missionary once entered the country ; on this occasion the people were warned that no females would be allowed to enter his house.

Marriage at *Loango* was a very simple affair : a man merely cast his eyes on a girl, of perhaps seven years of age, and when she arrived at the age of ten, little persuasion was needed to bring her to his dwelling. There were cases when men refused to sell their daughters at so tender an age. Should a girl have been seduced before her marriage, she had, as a matter of form, to confess this lapse to the chief and receive his pardon; the object being to prevent unlicensed freedom of intercourse, which would have menaced the well-being of the country, also to compel girls to recognize some sort of order.

Children were born nearly white, but became negroid in the space of two or three days; this at first puzzled the Portuguese, for when a child was born to a wife they had taken among the natives, they, at first, believed themselves the proud fathers; but the secret was out two days later.

There have been instances, when from a pure black pair, a child as white as any European was born. They were called *Dondos*, and were presented to the king, formed part of his retinue, and accompanied him everywhere; they were educated to become sorcerers. These albinos, as Dapper declares them to be, had the privilege of sitting in the presence of the king, and were always associated with every religious ceremony. The Portuguese placed considerable value on these albinos, in spite of their being inordinately lazy, and whenever chance offered, seized and transported them to Brazil, to be sold as slaves.

No stranger was ever allowed to be buried at Loango; if a European died, the people insisted that he should be taken away and buried at sea.

The king had the same respect paid him as though he were a god; he was given the title of *Samba* and *Pango*, signifying a god or divinity. The people implicitly believed that he could cause rain to fall; and, in the month of December when the earth was parched, they assembled together; and each man laying presents at the king's feet, supplicated him to bring them down this blessing. A day was then appointed for a gathering of all the chiefs with their followers who, fully equipped

for war, made obeisance to the monarch, seated
on the stool of state ; then ensued a terrific din
of the beating of drums, and blasting of trumpets,
the latter being made of elephant's tusks.   If rain
fell the same day, the festivities then reached a
stage of the greatest extravagance and licence.

The most solemn of all their ceremonies was in
connection with their drink, called *bonda* or
imbonda, an extraction from a root which was
allowed to ferment ; one of its effects being a
condition of intoxication, with complete loss of
the mental faculties ; under the effects of *bonda*
men claimed to foretell the future.

The Loanese asserted that no one died a natural
death ; it was either the result of some misdeed
the person had committed, or it was brought
about by an enemy.   If anyone had been devoured
by a tiger, the disaster was attributed to a *Dakkin*, or
a sorcerer who had been concealed in a tiger's skin ;
if a hut had been set alight, a *Mokisso*, or diviner,
had been neglected, and his wants unheeded.

When it was decided that an enquiry must be
made into the matter, a drink of *bonda* was
taken ; after which some nine or ten *Bonda* priests
were appointed to make further investigation.
This ceremony was held in the main street, about
the middle of the afternoon, when a complaint
was lodged against some suspected man.   The
accused then appeared with his family, for such
misconduct was rarely laid to the charge of a
single individual.   While the accusation was being
held, the priests kept up an incessant beating of a
small drum ; the accused and accuser each received
a potion of *bonda*, then returned to his place.

Among several tests used was when some of
the root from which *bonda* was brewed, was
thrown on the ground, and all the accused were

ordered to walk over it ; if one of them in his confused semi-intoxicated state fell, a great shout went up. The *Mokissos* were then thanked for having unravelled the truth, and received for their services all the clothes belonging to the accused; while the unhappy culprits were taken a short distance outside the village, and cut in pieces.

If the suspected was a rich man, he had the privilege of substituting a slave to this ordeal ; but if the slave failed in coming through it without evidence of guilt, the master had to take his place. Sometimes, however, he saved his life by the payment of a heavy fine. The poorer classes were, naturally, made the scapegoats, the priests regulating the ordeal in exactly the way which suited them best.

In Congo, if a woman allowed a man to take her pipe, and smoke it for a minute or two, she admitted his right to her favours. Another custom of the country was that a man could " sample " a woman for a considerable time without actually marrying her ; the same privilege was accorded a woman, who fully appreciated this period of freedom, which she was not too eager to relinquish for the bonds of matrimony, as once married she became little more than a slave. It was the woman who cooked the meals, who worked in the fields, while her husband lolled about or slept ; it was she who waited on, and served him ; the remains, only, of the repast were hers.

In cases of conjugal infidelity, a woman's lover was obliged to give her husband one of his slaves, or the equivalent. Infidelity committed outside the village was, in some places, Mr. H. Ward tells us, considered an assault ; the man, being the aggressor, therefore, alone was punished. Women were occasionally used as decoys to entrap men, who were then seized by the husband and, according to the law, sold by him into captivity or slavery. Marriage by purchase was also frequent, the market value of a woman being a small pig.

Among other authorities, Lopez observes that since the introduction of Christianity, in the 17th century, the population had considerably decreased; while polygamy existed they numbered hordes of people; and when a war was declared, the king had at his disposal a million fighting men. Modern writers still affirm that it was to polygamy that the African races owe their vigorous population, for it was only the strongest and fittest men who were able to buy wives.

It was customary for all the family to assemble at a funeral. The ceremonies commenced with the sacrifice of several fowls, the blood of which was sprinkled inside and outside of the hut. Then the body was placed on the top of the building so as to facilitate the escape of the soul; the fear being that the soul would remain behind, and trouble the people in some form or another : if the apparition of the soul was seen by anyone it was believed that he would immediately fall dead. This belief was so strongly inculcated into their minds that they did, occasionally, die from imagining they had met the ghost of the dead.

The ceremony of the fowls being ended, weeping and wailing commenced; if unable to produce tears, the mourners had recourse to a particular kind of snuff, which abundantly produced the desired effect. After a period of wailing, the scene was suddenly transformed into one of joy, the mourners eating and drinking the good things supplied by the bereaved ones. This, too, suddenly ceased, and the beating of drums called upon the multitude to dance; the ball began when a sufficiency of this excitement was produced; all the people adjourning into specified dark places, where a secret orgy began, with no fear of recognition. On these occasions, it was impossible for mothers to restrain their daughters; nor could even the slaves be prevented from rushing into this part of the festivities.

There was one remarkable custom associated with this last act of the orgies: should it be for the master of the house that these orgies were being held, the widow granted her favour to anyone who made request; the sole condition being, that not a word must be spoken while the pair were together. It will be noted that these debauches in the dark were in direct opposition to the Tahitians, to whom daylight was a *sine qua non*.

There was one law among these people which seemed the acme of senseless barbarity: it was forbidden to see the king eat or drink; if by the merest accident he had been observed, the penalty was instant death, whether it were a man, woman, child, animal, or bird. This law arose out of a superstition that if any creature witnessed such a sight, the king would shortly die. To kill the onlooker at once was therefore thought to be the means of redeeming his life.

One day, we are told, a boy of seven, son of a chief, fell asleep in the king's eating-room, and awoke just as the king was holding his drinking cup to his lips; the poor child had, consequently, his head split open with a hammer; and a few days later, his body was dragged by ropes to the public place of execution. Another little boy, running towards his father to embrace him, had, under similar circumstances, his head chopped in half, the priest rubbing the king's arm with the blood which had been spilt. Even the king's own

children were not exempt from this ghastly
fanaticism, for we hear that the son of a king,
aged eleven, chanced to enter the room while his
father was drinking. The boy was removed, fed
with the most appetizing food, the choicest drinks ;
and when he had finished the repast, he was cut
into quarters, which were carried round, and
exhibited throughout the village. Dogs and cats
met with a similar fate.

The date of any event dated from the number
of seasons since the death of any notorious person.
There was a beginning, a middle, an end of a day :
a new and a full moon ; beyond this, days or
years were devoid of meaning. In the same way,
the age of five or six meant reaching maturity ;
after this period there were no such things as
stages, or years of age.

Priests, known by the name of *Gangas*, signifying gods of the earth, had a high-priest called
Ganza Kitorna ; it was to this god they attributed
the produce of the earth : he claimed to be
immune from death by natural causes. When,
either owing to old age or disease, he found himself nearing his end, he disclosed to the successor
he had chosen, the secret of his power to induce
fertility, to yield abundant harvests ; this done,
he was publicly strangled. The people were fully
convinced that if the office of high-priest should
fall into abeyance, the whole land would become
sterile, and all humanity shortly perish.

In his *Voice from the Congo*, H. Ward says that
their religion was a belief in good and evil spirits ;
but since the former did not interfere with their
happiness, they were practically ignored. It was
the evil spirits who were in constant attendance,
perpetually fermenting trouble and upsetting
matters—whom they sought to propitiate rather

than worship, for they were in perpetual dread of
the activities of these malevolent beings. The
witch-doctor was the medium of this propitiation
between man and the spirit world ; it was he who
by counter charms negatived the power of these
evil ones ; moreover, he was a salutary observer
into the results of cause and effect, as well as the
present and future.

The act of snapping the fingers was said to
have the certain effect of dispelling any evil spirit
which might have been inadvertently alluded to ;
also, by some obscure reasoning, the right hand,
being the stronger and more useful, was regarded
as masculine, the left hand being feminine.

The sensation of being pointed at was objec-
tionable to a native, for it suggested the trans-
mission of an evil wish ; also, when asked, a
native had a strong objection to giving his name.
Among some tribes, in spite of the scorching sun,
both the eyebrows and eyelashes were pulled out ;
others were also known to shave their heads.

For the sake of the hair or bristles on an elephant's tail, which were used as ornaments by
the women, it is said that hunters would lie in
wait for the animal to pass through a narrow
defile ; and when is was unable to turn, they cut
off the tail ; some of these gallant hunters would
even dock the animal of its tail while it was
grazing, and escape from the animal's fury by
running away in zigzag fashion.

These may be mere hunters' yarns, although
there is no doubt that elephants were very numerous before the advent of the professional ivory
hunters, and accustomed to the natives, to the
extent of familiarity; for Lopez recounts that an
elephant was known to approach the village,
and out of sheer mischief or fun, lift up with his

trunk some man he met, swing him round, finally
gently placing him on his feet. We have it also
from Dapper, that if an elephant had killed a
man, in consequence of being wounded by him,
he first dug a hole with his tusks, then buried him,
finally reverently covering him over with earth.

Regarding the efficacy of the written symbol,
Mungo Park relates that when in *Koolkarro* " my
landlord brought out his writing-board that I
might write him a *saphie*, to protect him from
wicked men. I wrote the board full, from top
to bottom, on both sides : and my landlord, to
be certain of having the whole force of the charm,
washed the writing from the board into a *calabash* :
and having said a few prayers over it, drank this
powerful draught ; after which, lest a single word
should escape, he licked the board until it was
quite dry."

Before concluding the Congo proper, it will be
interesting to hear something of its near neighbours, especially the *Anzikos*, and the *Jaggas* ;
with both these people, human flesh was sold in
the market ; this flesh was either the remains of
slaves captured in war, or possibly the slaves of
their own caste, who were considered sufficiently
well fattened for the market. Indeed, slaves
themselves if they became weary of life, or to
show their contempt of death, occasionally offered
themselves to provide a feast for the king. One
reads of people eating strangers ; but these people
of *Anzikos* were unique, as their cannibalism
extended to their own tribe, not excepting their
parents.

The *Jaggas* inhabited a vast area reaching south
to the Hottentot tribes, and as far north-east as
Abyssinia. As a tribal mark, they seared lines
down their cheeks with a hot iron ; further they

had a custom of showing only the whites of the
eyes, covering the iris with the eyelids, thus
succeeding in making themselves horrible and
repulsive. The most redoubtable adversaries of
these wild forest nomads, were the so-called
Amazons, in no way similar to the Amazons of
South America or the Philippines, but a race of
female warriors who inhabited *Monomotapa*, on
the frontier of Jagga. These women accompanied
the men in their constant raids ; but any children
born during an expedition were destroyed ; owing
to this custom they left no posterity.

The explanation given of this infanticide was
that they could not be troubled to bring up children, and moreover they would always be a hin-
drance in their constant wanderings in search of
food, and their incursions into villages. To
counterbalance the death-rate, they raided a
village, seized the youth of both sexes, assimilating
them into their tribe, while their parents were
eaten. Both the boys and girls had a ring
round their necks until they had proved their
worth and courage, when they were freed and
became entitled to full membership. These *Jaggas*
seem to have been the lowest type of humanity.

Just as in Europe, one may see a broken column
over a grave, symbolical of a broken life ; so, at
some places in the Congo, the shattered pots at
the desert well would, for the same reason, be
piled up to cover a grave.

FIJI

FIJIANS had many customs which distinguished them from their nearer neighbours; and it has been thought that with their dark skins and mops of black hair, they had originally been mixed with darker nations of Asia. Their chiefs were considered to be of divine origin, their dignity being conferred by the gods. In *Somosomo* the kings only were permitted to use umbrellas, but as a mark of special favour this privilege was shared by the two high-priests. His Majesty's thumb-nail was also, as a sign of superiority, allowed to grow an inch longer than mere mortals'.

The day on which tributes were paid, was held as a high festival; whales' teeth, cowrie necklets, tortoise-shell hair-pins (eighteen inches long), cocks' tail feathers, etc., were all *en évidence* on that gala day. Women's coiffure had been specially treated beforehand for months, as were men's beards. The king and his suite graciously received the tributes, which were presented with a song and a dance; those who—proud of their capital—had paid theirs were afterwards entertained at a feast provided by the king. Among other forms of payment were floor-mats—for which they were famous—fishing-nets, weapons of war, etc.; the list included " turtles and women " ; no wonder the king was gracious, and in high good humour.

The characteristics of this people were extreme caution (which they had doubtless learnt from experience) and astuteness. Anything of a slight was rarely forgiven, although little reference might be made to it at the moment; but some stick or stone would be put in such a position that it could be constantly seen, and would serve as a perpetual

FIJIAN CANOE.

reminder of the grievance, until it could be avenged.

Etiquette, or custom, prevented brothers or sisters, first cousins, fathers and sons-in-law, and many such relations either to speak to one another, or to eat from the same dish ; this custom extended to husbands and wives.

Marriage was merely a contract. Until a woman became a man's property she was as free as men, and if she had a temporary liaison, both parties could find a public absolution if they confessed their transgression. Indeed, this was said to render them safer from any future sudden death which might be visited on them in consequence of this amour. Intermarriage within prohibited degrees was strictly adhered to ; the ideal mating was supposed to be between the children of parents who were brother and sister, as the offspring were believed to be sturdier and truer to the Race. In fact, these children claimed to be married by Divine right ; moreover they claimed the rites of this marriage, in addition to those of their marriage to another individual.

Some children were betrothed during their infancy ; the girl was literally " given away " by her mother's brother in the form of a deposit ; gifts were also tendered to the child's parents, while the uncle was presented with a club wherewith to guard the " property." Up to the time they were about sixteen years old, the couple neither addressed one another, nor sat in each other's company ; finally the bride was tattooed, which was followed by the spreading of the mats, and their friends seeing them installed thereon. The following day the important rite took place of tying and knotting of the shorter skirt, the symbol of womanhood—this public tying and knotting was the woman's marriage lines, as legal

and binding as any document. The bridal couple
were then enclosed in the hut for four days, food
being brought to them by friends and neighbours.
When this honeymoon was over, the man never
again occupied the same hut as his wife ; instead
of which he slept in the men's hall. The pair,
however, met on common ground during any other
hours of the day.

In some places, when the marriage had reached
completion, a large bunch of the bride's hair, over
her temples, was cut off. Should an owl fly over her
husband's home, it was an omen that he would
become the father of a son. The naming of
children was possibly some peculiarity in the child,
some incident connected with its birth, or a record
of family triumphs, perhaps even a name denoting
the folly and downfall of their enemies. One of an
infant's first lessons was to strike its mother, lest
it should grow up a coward. Children were also
easily taught to kick and tread upon the dead
bodies of their enemies, as well as the children who
were slain.

To a certain extent some of the people had
preserved the tradition of the same ancestry, and
although separated, in various parts of the
islands, still claimed kinship with each other.
This clanship was celebrated by visits of one group
to another ; on these occasions the guests had the
privilege of a hospitality, which permitted them
to help themselves to all coveted possessions—
without exception. At a future date, on a return
visit, the visitors could, in their turn, help themselves. It must have been a very costly entertainment, for on each occasion each lost most of
his goods and chattels.

Infanticide was extremely common among the
Fijians ; jealousy and revenge being one reason

given ; shortage of food another ; but all children thus destroyed were females. Yet, with a strange contradiction, they frequently adopted orphans, upon whom they lavished far more affection than upon their own offspring.

The old and infirm were treated with such scant kindness that they frequently implored their children to murder them. More especially, as it was believed they entered a future existence at the same period in which they left this one ; thus they would be secure from extreme old age in a future world. Nor were the sick, unless of high rank, or having rendered great services, any better off ; for after a few days they were either left to perish with hunger, or were put out of the way.

When a Chief was dead or dying, it was a very different matter ; his relations were immediately notified, and should he be a powerful ruler, the principal men of his kingdom came to pay their respects, bringing with them some present. As in the East, there was a scene of public wailing ; the women asking the dead such questions as, " Why did you die ? Were you weary of us ? We are around you now. Why do you close your eyes upon us ? " We are told of a child of rank dying, who was under the charge of the Queen of Somo-somo. The body was placed in a box and suspended from the beam of the principal *lure* (a praying house in which the priests lived) ; the best of food was brought it daily for some months, the bearers waiting respectfully, as long as an ordinary person would take in consuming a meal ; at the end of which time they would clap their hands in the same way as a chief when he had finished eating, and retire.

The grave in which a chief was buried was lined with mats, upon which were laid the strangled bodies of several of his wives, and over these was placed the chief; cloth and mats covered the bodies, and earth filled in the grave. After these hapless women had been strangled, they were well oiled, their hair dressed and ornamented; and vermillion or "tumeric" powder spread on their faces. Common graves were only edged round with stones; on some graves were cairns of stones, or baskets of ornaments to please the one who lay below.

There were several modes of divination, one being that after the priest had delivered his message to the gods, he shook with great violence a bunch of rather dry cocoa-nuts; if they all fell off, it was a sign that a sick child would recover; if any remained—it would die. Another method employed was for the priests to seat themselves on the ground, their legs stretched out, with a small club placed between them. If the right leg trembled first it was a good omen, but if the left, it was an indication of evil. An omen was sometimes judged according as to whether a man, holding a certain sort of stick, sneezed out of his right or left nostril. Apart from the seer of Fiji, there was the professional dreamer; it was, however, apparently useless to consult these gentlemen unless one was prepared to pay a goodly sum.

Superstitions were abundant; if rats scratched at the mould of a woman's grave, it might be taken that she had been unchaste. Large shooting-stars were said to be gods; smaller ones, the departed souls of men. Among other traditions there was one which accounted for universal death. When the first man, father of the human race, was being buried by his sons, a god passed by, who said, "Do not inter him. Dig up the body again." The reply was, that as the body had

Fijian Police.

already been dead four days it had become corrupt and must be buried. "Not so," said the god; "disinter him, and I promise you he shall live again." The deceased man's sons refused to believe these words, and, perceiving their obstinacy and disobedience, the god said, "Had you dug up your ancestor, you would have found him alive; and yourselves also, as you passed from this world, should have been buried as bananas are, for the space of four days; after which you should have been dug up, not rotten, but ripe. But now, as a punishment for your disobedience, you shall die and rot." "Oh!" the Fijians used afterwards to lament, "Oh! that these children had dug up the body."

Cannibalism was rife in the island; the gods, who were declared to have voracious appetites, were said to gloat over *bakolo* (human flesh set apart for eating), and it is very certain that the Fijians gloated no less. On the building of a *lure*, or the launching of a large canoe, or taking down the mast of the canoe of a chief who had come to visit them, human bodies were sometimes eaten. Mr. Williams, the missionary, says that he never heard of this delectable food being eaten raw. As in other countries, captives, and the slain of either sex, usually provided these abominable banquets, but in this respect they were not over-particular; those who escaped shipwreck were also usually eaten, but individuals who died a natural death were always buried. When speaking of cannibalism, a Fijian said that before the intro-duction of pigs, there were times when he had an uncontrollable desire for flesh; when this lust entered into their souls it was a case of unrest, and when once acquired it was not easy to break the habit.

Each island in Fiji had its own gods and superstitions. The name of the god most known was
Ndengei, who seems to have impersonated eternity ;
some traditions picture him with the head and
part of a body of a serpent, the rest of his form
being stone, the emblem of the ever-existing. His
abode was in a gloomy cavern near the north-east
end of *Vita-levu* ; he seems hardly to have been
an attractive personage, as he showed no interest
in anyone but his attendant, Uto ; indeed his
only signs of life were answering his priest, eating,
and moving his position from side to side. But
although he ranked as the most important of the
gods, he was worshipped less than others, and
had but few temples.

Some of their other gods had the shapes of
monsters ; among these were *Rokomoutu*, a son of
Ndengei's sister, who insisted upon being born from
her elbow. He showed his natural benevolence by
threatening to devour his mother and friends, unless
he was regarded as a god. *Thangawalu* was a
giant from birth, and quickly grew to the height
of sixty feet.

Ra Nambasanga had two bodies—one male, the
other female. *Mbakandroti* was the Fijian's war-
god ; it was believed that were he to use only
the pandanus leaf, he would be immune from all
human attack. *Ndauthina* was given to stealing
women of rank and beauty, by night or torch-light.
Mbatimona was the brain-eater.

The Fijians regarded certain stones and war-
clubs as the shrines of their gods ; a few men,
certain fish, birds, plants, were also believed to
have gods dwelling in them, such as the hawk,
shark, eel, etc. Anyone worshipping a particular
god had to refrain from eating the animal in which
he was believed to dwell.

If a priest was also a doctor, a number of hand-clubs, necklaces of flowers, etc., paid as fees, were collected in the *lures* ; portions of victims slain in war were also often hung up in bunches. There were priestesses in Fiji, but few of these had *lures* erected for them, as they were not considered of sufficient importance.

Beyond the planting of wild yams, and the wreckages of strange canoes on their shore, the Fijians had little belief in the benevolence of their gods, although they occasionally presented thank-offerings on their recovery from sickness and disaster in the shape of clubs, spears, etc.

No woman was ever permitted to enter a *lure*, and from some, dogs were also excluded. To sit on the threshold of a temple was always *taboo* except to the chiefs ; persons of distinction " strode over " any spot dedicated to the gods ; the remainder crawled over on their hands and knees. It was believed that sometimes the gods assumed human form and could be seen by men ; they were generally supposed to appear in the likeness of some well-known person. Should any-one meet a god, he was expected when again walking over the same spot to throw on it a few leaves or blades of grass, to show that the remembrance had not passed from his mind.

The law of *taboo* in all parts of the South Seas was the essence of the despotic rule among the chiefs ; everything of value which they wished to keep exclusively for themselves came under this heading. In *Mbakandroti* the *taboo* secured to the priests all the pigs which had only one ear ; but as this was of small profit to them, this was made to mean—all swine which had one ear shorter or narrower than the other.

Any gloomy forests or dark caverns were peopled

by the Fijians with invisible spirits on the alert to injure them ; at one particular entrance of some gloomy defile it was believed that *Lewa-levu*—" the Great Woman "—was waiting to pounce on any particular men who took her fancy.   They also believed that dead spirits were able to trouble the living, more especially when they were asleep ; the ones they most feared were the spirits of dissolute women, those who died in childbirth, or men who had been slain.   Some, also, believed that a man had two spirits ; his shadow was called " *the dark spirit* " and remained near the place where he had died.   These places were to be avoided, more particularly when it rained, otherwise the moans of the spirit could be heard as it sat up, trying to get some relief by resting its head in the palms of its hands.   Others declared the moans were caused by the soul of the murderer striking down the soul of the victim, whenever he attempted to rise.

The Paradise of the Fijians was in *Mburotu*, where they enjoyed abundantly everything which they had relished best on earth ; but there were many trials and ordeals before they arrived at their Elysium ; replies to questions as to their fitness, and whether they had fully subscribed to the rites and ceremonies of their tribe.   The ghost of a bachelor had to take special precautions to elude the clutches of " the Great Woman."   The club of the Soul-destroyer, and other dangers, had also to be escaped ; and according to their belief, few, alas ! arrived at immortality.

GREECE

THE original founder of Athens was Cecrops, who, among other wise laws for the welfare of the people, instituted the law of marriage. About 600 B.C. Athens became a republic ; but it suffered many reverses ; amongst others, it was twice burnt to ashes by the Persians. Years rolled on, and after the yoke of Macedon had laid its claws on the Greeks, it was invaded by the Romans ; while in the third century, Alaric and his Vandals displaced the Romans. Finally, about 1450, the Turks took possession of Athens, and did not slacken their hold, until the Spirit of Greece had practically ceased to exist.

*　　*　　*　　*

The age of marriage differed widely under different rulers ; Aristotle considered thirty-seven a suitable age, while Plato and Hesiod were in favour of thirty " since strength and prudence to the State belong." Among maids, the age was much earlier, although rather later than in other nations ; Aristotle declaring in preference of eighteen, and Hesiod fifteen.

The Lacedæmon men were compelled to marry before they reached a given age, for not desiring to increase the population legitimately was considered a heinous crime, indicating a want of patriotism. In the event of their failing to conform to this injunction, certain penalties were inflicted ; among others, they were obliged to run naked round the Public Forum, singing an appropriate song, the words of which would not only increase the enormity of their offence, but make themselves an object of ridicule. Another punishment for abstaining from marriage, was being dragged round an altar by a number of women, beating the culprits all the while with their fists. We hear, too, of a famous Captain of Sparta, insulted in the Public Assembly, by a youth of Lacedæmon, for preferring to remain unshackled from the fetters of matrimony.

These people were forbidden to marry any of their kindred ; no objection, however, was made in the case of a collateral relative ; hence nephews married their aunts, and uncles their nieces. Men were in some places permitted to marry their half-sisters by the same father.

They bathed their newly-born children in new wine, as this was said to induce convulsions in the sickly, and only hardy children were wanted in Greece. They also obliged all fathers to carry their new-born children to a convention of " the gravest Men in their own Tribe." If these found them strong and lusty, they gave orders that they should be educated by the State, and a certain measure of land was portioned out to them for their maintenance. Should they, on the contrary, be pronounced sickly or deformed, they were thrown into a deep cavern, it being considered they would grow up burdens both to themselves and to the general community.

Winter was usually believed the most propitious season for matrimony, especially the month of January, or at the conjunction of the Sun with the phase of the Moon, when the Greeks celebrated the marriage of their gods, believing that in the matter of generation, the full Moon was a powerful agent. In ancient times, women were obtained by purchase, without a marriage portion, the husband presenting his wife's relations with sundry gifts, of more or less value, which were

called her dowry.   But Lycurgas and Solon, fearing
lest women should become too masterful over
their husbands, and marry for gain, not love,
limited these gifts to "a little inconsiderable
household stuff, and three new suits of clothing."

It was a custom among Athenian maidens, to
offer their hair to one of their Deities ; when they
arrived at a marriageable age they were also
presented to Diana, the Goddess of Chastity, and
laid at her feet an offering of little baskets of
curiosities in order to gain permission to depart
from her allegiance of followers.

Before a marriage took place, the house was
festooned with garlands ; a pestle was tied to the
door, while a servant carried a sieve, and the bride
an earthen vessel of parched barley, a symbol of
her obligation to discharge her household duties.
She was, as a rule, conveyed to her husband's
house in a chariot ; the time, we are told, being
evening, in order the better to conceal her blushes.
Torches were carried in front of the chariot, which
was sometimes escorted by singers and dancers,
the bride being seated between her husband and
one of his best friends.   Upon their arrival the
axle-tree of the carriage wheel was burnt, symbolizing that the bride would not be returning to
her father's house.

One of Solon's laws was that an Athenian heiress
must, in order to retain the estates in the family,
marry her nearest of kin.   Should her husband
be unable to provide her with the necessary offspring, she was entitled to summon the aid of his
nearest relation.   Men were compelled, if their
wives were heiresses, to share her nuptial couch
for at least three nights a month ; and above all,
under no consideration was an Athenian woman
to "marry her self into an exotick Family."

Maids were not allowed to marry without the consent of their parents (nor indeed were men) ; if fatherless they were disposed of in marriage by their brothers ; or when orphans and penniless, their nearest of kin had either to marry them or settle on them a sum of money. Should their fathers have rendered service to their country, they were frequently looked after by the State. Sometimes Athenian children, like the Lacedæmons, if physically unfit were killed, or left exposed in desert places.

In later days the Athenians exceeded any other people in the number of their gods ; their festivals were in like proportion, when "the Labourers rested from their Works, the Tradesmen from their Employments, the Mourners intermited their Sorrows."

All theatres were dedicated to Bacchus and Venus, the gods of sport and pleasure ; to Bacchus they are said to have owed their origin ; an ivy leaf being the symbol of that Deity.

In the *Bibliothèque des Antiques* we learn, that in Athens the right hand of suicides was cut off ; and although the body was interred, the usual funeral ceremonies were omitted.

At Athens there was a certain day appointed at one of their feasts, when the hair of their children was cut off and sacrificed to Diana. The Athenian laws did not permit the sacrifice of men, but among the Carthaginians it was regarded as a holy rite ; so that some of them permitted their sons to be offered to Saturn ; this custom at last overspread all nations, amongst others the Greeks. Ovid speaks of the women, who accompanied their fathers or husbands in battle, as putting on their finest dresses and ornaments previous to an engagement, in order to attract the notice of the conqueror if taken prisoner.

Diogenes Laertius, in his life of Epimenides, says that during the life of that great philosopher, a fearful pestilence broke out in Athens, and that none of their gods to whom they sacrificed seemed able to help them. Epimenides therefore advised that some sheep should be brought to theAreopagus and let loose, and when they lay down they should be sacrificed to the god whose temple or altar they were nearest. But we are further told that in that age there were fewer altars, consequently the sheep were not near any, which obliged what the author calls " anonymous altars " to be built, on each of which was written the inscription, " To the unknown God."

Pliny, quoting from *Isigonus*, says that among the Triballians and Illyrians there were certain enchanters, " who with their looks could bewitch and kill those whom they beheld for a considerable time, especially if they did so with angry eyes."

The Greeks dealt largely in love potions ; among other ingredients used to gain the heart of their beloved was the blood of doves, the bones of snakes, and the feathers of " Scritch-Owls." Some of these potions were so poisonous that instead of inflaming the blood of the " scornful Maid " they unfortunately deprived her of her reason. Love-sick boys also tied garlands and flowers on the door of their lover's house. Should these be found untied, it might be taken as a sign that their passion was returned. Great significance was attached to uneven numbers, more especially to the number three, which possessing as it does a Beginning, Middle, and End, " it seems natural to signify all Things in the World," and was particularly acceptable to the gods.

The *Rhodians* had a curious custom among their marriage rites, of sending for the bride by means of

the town-crier. When they arrived at the bridegroom's house, a grand feast had been provided
with the purpose of announcing the marriage,
refreshing their guests, and doing honour to the
gods. A boy, crowned with acorns and thorn-
boughs, produced a basket of bread, and sang,
" I have left the worse and found the better."
After the bridal pair had been conducted to their
chamber the bride was obliged to bathe her feet
with water, brought by a boy who was connected
with one of the two families. Their friends now
escorted them, by the light of several torches, to
their bridal couch, when the bride's mother tied
her daughter's " Hair-lace " round one of the
torches ; at length the wedded pair were left alone,
though still serenaded outside the door by their
friends, who returned again the following morning.
According to the Athenian law they were obliged
to eat a quince between them, to show that their
conversation would be agreeable and har-
monious.

Grecian laws on divorce differed considerably :
Cretans were allowed to dispose of their wives,
should they be in fear of too large families.
Spartans, on the contrary, rarely divorced their
wives. Athenian women were allowed greater
licence. We read of some remarkable facts, as
when Antiochus was violently enamoured of his
mother-in-law, and by his father's consent, made
her his wife. Another custom, not infrequent in
some parts of Greece, was husbands borrowing one
another's wives. Socrates lent his wife Xantippe
to Alcibiades. Indeed Lycurgas, the Spartan law-
giver, thought the " best Expedient against
Jealousie, was to allow Man the Freedom of
imparting the use of their Wives to whom they
should think fit." Not, however, in the case of

kings, whose blood should be unmixed so as to keep it pure.

In regard to irregular infidelity, which was not of mutual consent, as long as the Nation kept to their ancient laws, such iniquity was regarded as unthinkable. When Geradas, a primitive Spartan, was asked what punishment should be meted out for infidelity, he replied " That the Offender must pay to the Plaintiff, a Bull with a Neck so long as that he might reach over the Mountain Taygetus, and drink of the River Eurotas that runs on the other Side." The enquirer answered, " Why, 'tis impossible to find such a Bull," to which Geradas smilingly replied, " 'Tis just as possible to find an Adulterer in Sparta."

In some parts of Greece the penalty for infidelity was very severe : the delinquent might be muti-lated, stoned to death, or have his eyes gouged out. A much milder form of punishment was being covered by wool, as an indication that the wearer was too " soft " to resist temptation. He was also deprived of all rights as a citizen, or of managing a public business. Women guilty of infidelity, were subjected to the harsh punishment of never again being allowed to appear in fine raiment.

Laws also in regard to thieves were stringent, especially those who conducted their thefts at night. Moreover, precautions were taken in regard to " He, who makes search for *Theeves* in another's House, must have only a thin Garment hanging loose about him." Among other laws, no one might become an Actor before he was thirty ; others have declared the age to be forty.

Punishments varied greatly according to different magistrates. In spite of their often brutal treat-ment of infidelity, the ancient Greeks were lenient in the extreme to concubinage, and were allowed to keep as many wives as they chose ; although concubines were always considered as inferior to wives. They were, as a rule, captives, or had been procured through influence or money. Dr. Potter tells us how children shared in the disgrace and punishment of their father for evil doing ; this punishment was declared to be through no spirit of revenge but of justice ; but as the children had profited by their father's good fortune, so they should share in his losses and dishonour.

Entertainments in the primitive days of Greece were simple in the extreme : not more than four or five persons were present. It would have shown a great breach of good manners, had the assembled guests sat down immediately at the table. Before doing so, the room and furniture would have to be commented upon. Relations frequently came uninvited. Some of these unbidden guests went by the name of " Flies " (Latin), and they were referred to by Roman and Greek authorities, and described by Horus Apollo as "the Hieroglyphick of an *impudent* Man, because that Insect, being beaten away, still returns again." Men and women were never invited together, as no woman was ever present at entertainments unless her nearest relations were present.

The ancient Greeks " sat at Meat " in three kinds of seats : the first one could hold two persons ; in them sat the most humble of the guests ; on the second one each person sat upright with a stool at his feet ; the third had a slightly sloping back, and on it sat the most honoured guest. Later, when the Greeks degenerated, and became more luxurious, it was common for beds to be moved into the banqueting halls " in order to drink with more ease."

Strangers were treated with great courtesy :

" Put the bewildered Traveller in his way, and be hospitable to Strangers," but " Sojourners " at public processions were commanded to carry " little Vessels fram'd after the model of a Boat, and their Daughters Waterpots with Umbrellas," to shield them from the weather.

Omens were held in great esteem with the Greeks, these being so innumerable that only a few can be given. Lightning was regarded, as were most of the forces of Nature, with the greatest fear ; so much did they fear it, that Pliny says it was worshipped to lessen its malign effect, which form of worship was that they hissed and whistled at it. When any place had been struck by lightning, an altar was erected and a lamb sacrificed. Others believed lightning to be a good omen, when it was seen on the right side, and only a bad one when seen on the left. Those who were killed by it were considered to have rendered themselves obnoxious to the gods ; and were either buried apart, lest they contaminated the ashes of other men, or allowed to decay in the place where they fell.

Omens which came from the East were good, as all the principles of life and heat come from there ; but omens that appeared from the West were bad, insomuch as the Sun declines in that direction.

The Rev. S. S. Wilson, in his *Sixteen Years in Malta and Greece*, observes that " when the right eye winks and the left recoils," it was a good sign. Sneezing was considered to foretell disease for which reason, in order to avert the mischief, it was recommended to say " God bless you." Ammian composed an epigram on one who had a long nose :

" His long-beak'd Snout, at such a distance lyes
From his dull Ears, that he ne're hears it Sneeze ;
And therefore never do's he say, *God* bless."

Others declared that if anyone sneezed at the table while they were clearing it, it was esteemed unlucky ; or if another sneezed on his left hand ; but if on the right one, it was a fortunate omen. Pliny declared that the Thessalian magicians destroyed whole harvests by speaking well of them. Amulets, too, against evil spirits were much in request. Should anyone be seized by a violent distemper, it was usual to hang over his door a branch of thyme and laurel, as likely to keep off evil spirits.

Some dreams were imputed to the God of Sleep, whose Abode, Ovid tells us, was " in a Den as dark as Hell," and around him lay " swarms of Dreams of all sorts and sizes," which he sent forth when and where it pleased him.

In the earliest ages the Greeks had neither idols nor altars, but worshipped their gods on the top of high mountains, the reason being that it was nearest the heavens, and consequently easier for gods to hear their prayers.   Later, they frequently built their temples on the summits of the mountains ; temples were also said to have been originally erected as monuments of their departed.

The dead were held in great veneration, and to the living was entrusted the honour of their memory.   Should they fail in this respect great would be their dishonour ; indeed Solon went so far as to leave nothing to chance, but to have such punished.   How understandable was this attitude of the Greeks, when one realizes their belief that the soul could not enter the Elysian shades, but wandered in gloom and desolation until their bodies were laid to rest in the earth.   Should they indeed remain unburied, one hundred years must elapse before they were able to enter " the

Receptacle of Ghosts," which would keep them
secure from the Furies.

Those who had betrayed their Nation were first
stoned to death and then cast out of their country
unburied.

To be drowned at sea would be naturally one
of the Greeks' greatest terrors. To try to obviate
the consequences, they attached, whenever it was
possible, valuable pieces of jewellery to the body,
with the understanding that he who found the
treasure and buried the body with proper funeral
rites, might keep at least part of the reward.
In every case it was believed that the Deities
would inflict severe retribution on anyone who,
finding the body, allowed it to remain unburied.
They were, also, ordered not "to speak evil of
the Dead, no not, tho' their Children provoke you."

Young men who died in the flower of their
youth were buried in the "Morning Twilight,"
for their death was considered as such a fearful
calamity that it would have been thought indecor-
ous, almost impious, to have subjected them to the
full blaze of the Sun.

However contradictory the authorities, it seems
conclusive the ancient Greeks originally buried
their dead ; but later, mainly for the reason that
after the soul's departure, fire was the greatest
purifier, they burnt their dead. An additional
reason being given, that the soul had an easier
means of escape, when it was separated from the
grosser elements. It was this belief that made the
natives of India erect a funeral pyre as soon as
was possible, thus setting free the soul. Occasions
indeed occurred, when people were, by their own
desire, placed on the funeral pyre before death
had actually taken place.

Dr. Potter tells us that the Greeks frequently

cut their hair, and threw it on the dead body, or on to the funeral " pile " ; and that Electris found fault with Helena for sparing her hair, thereby defrauding the dead. There was also an ancient custom for procuring mourning women over sixty years of age, at their funerals. Jeremy called for " *the Mourning women, that they may make haste, and take up awailing for us, that our Eyes may run down with Tears, and our Eye-lids gush out with Water.*"

They believed in two Mansions after Death ; the one on the right hand was full of rapture and delights ; the one on the left was, on the contrary, an infernal region : " for the Souls of wicked Wretches." The Furies were always trying to hurry the souls of the departed into this place of anguish, that they, as well as those whose rightful place it was, might be tormented.

It was customary to lay out the dead near the entrance of the house, so that any who passed might be able to observe whether there were marks of such injury as might cause death. They had, in common with the Jews, and many other nations, a horror of being contaminated after washing a corpse. In ancient times, children under forty days were buried within the threshold of the house. As a money security it was permissible in Athens to seize a dead body for debt, and to deprive it of the honour of burial until the debt was paid.

Previous to interment a coin was inserted into the mouth of the corpse : this was believed to be Charon's price for ensuring a safe passage of a soul over the Infernal River.

The Reception of Captain Cook in Hapaee (Hawaii).

Facing page 71

HAWAIIAN OR SANDWICH ISLANDS

THIS group of islands in the North Pacific Ocean, lies about 2000 miles to the westward of San Francisco on the American coast. There is reason to believe they were discovered by Juan Gaetana, a Spaniard, in about 1550; but it was not until over 200 years later that Captain Cook made their existence known.

It has been assumed that the people were, in the first instance, one of the scattered remnants of the exodus in about the 4th century, of a race that overran Malaya; others drifted to Fiji and the Polynesian Islands. It is also suggested that in about the 10th century, through some unconscious urge, a further migration took place from the Friendly Islands by way of Polynesia, that found its way to the Hawaiian Islands; these last being cousins, centuries removed, seemed subconsciously to have recognized this kinship. Accordingly they actually made many visits to each other over a distance of about 2500 miles in rickety canoes, swept hither and thither by the strong equatorial currents, out of sight of land and guided it is not known by what, carrying food and water for a journey which must have taken them at least forty days.

The principal island of the group, the one on which the King eventually dwelt, was called Wahoo (the latest spelling of this being Oahu), the capital being Honolulu; while the largest island known as Owhyhee, now spelt Hawaii, was the island on which Captain Cook was massacred in 1778. One of the islands named Molokai is that on which still exists the famous leper settlement, with whose name Father Damien was so heroically associated.

When Captain Cook visited these islands,
Tamaahmaah (spelt in different ways) was king ;
one of his attendants carried a feather fan to brush
away the flies ; another attendant carried his spit-
box, which was set around with human teeth.
He was always accompanied by his principal chiefs,
and all sat down together at meals, the main
article of diet being *Taro* pudding (Poe), a root
baked in a pit with hot stones. It was of the
consistency of paste, and was picked out of a pot
with closed fingers and drawn up to the mouth,
after which the fingers were licked clean. There
would be a two or three finger Poe, classified
according to its consistency. Besides this delicacy,
salt fish was served and pork consecrated for the
king's sole use.

Whenever his Majesty passed the people were
obliged to uncover their heads and shoulders ; the
same ceremony took place whenever anyone
passed or entered the King's entrance, or any
house which he had ever entered. When the
King's food was carried from the cooking-house,
the bearer of the dish called out " Noho," meaning
literally " sit down," and everyone within hearing
had to squat on his haunches. This ceremony
would have been peculiarly trying, it being
necessary to bring the water from the mountains,
a distance of five miles, had not the calabash
carriers who were obliged to call out " Noho," run
past as quickly as they were able, so as not to
detain the people.

When the King's brother died there was public
mourning ; the natives cut off their hair, and went
about completely nude ; indeed many of them,
more especially the women, disfigured themselves
by knocking out their front teeth and branding
their faces with red hot stones. A scene of great

licentiousness also took place, from which, however, the Queen and the deceased's widow were exempt.

There were only two classes, the chiefs and the people ; the chiefs owned all the land and the priests collected the taxes. This took place at harvest time, November, and was the occasion of many festivities—dancing and games, which lasted a month. Their house of worship was called *Morai*, in which the priests lived, and during the tax-collecting festivities the King remained in the *Morai*.

Archibald Campbell, who resided in Wahoo (Oahu) in 1810, says that a curious ceremony took place before the King entered this *Morai*. He was obliged to stand until three spears were rapidly darted at him ; the first he had to catch with his hand, and with it ward off the other two. Should any unforeseen accident occur, and the King lost his life, it was merely put down to one of those evils to which human mortals are prone.

According to Captain Vancouver, this King Tamaahmaah was so dexterous with a spear, that he once saw him in a sham fight ward off six spears closely following one another. Three he caught with his hand, two he broke by parrying them with his spear ; the sixth, by a slight inclination of the body, passed harmlessly.

The King had two Queens, who were sisters. It is recorded that his eldest son, Tianna, had been put to death, in consequence of a liaison with one of his wives. To make kites was one of Queen Tamena's favourite amusements ; these gigantic kites were made 15 or 16 feet long. This lady preserved the bones of her father, wrapt up in a piece of cloth, and slept with them by her side. Another of the Queen's amusements was to make

her attendant women drunk ; by the end of this
entertainment she was in a more intoxicated state
than they.

The natives were described as of moderate
height, stout and robust ; their skin of a nut-brown
colour and they were extremely cleanly. Bathing
was the remedy for all their ails. Their dwellings
consisted of simple square huts with thatched
roofs ; there being no windows, their only light
was obtained through the door. The inside was
an empty space, but the walls were decorated with
cooking utensils. On a platform about a couple of
feet high, and covered with native mats, one part
of the household slept ; the remainder found room,
as best they could, on the ground at the other end
of the hut. Women only ate in this house, which
was probably while they were cooking. Men had
their meals apart from the women, and for them a
separate eating-house was required, which was also
shared by the men of several families.

Fish was mostly consumed raw, fresh out of the
salt water, and was supposed to promote a sort of
scaly scurf on the skin. These people were expert
fishermen, especially with nets ; they also caught
fish by poisonous herbs, a device known universally. For lighting purposes they used the " candle-
nut," the fruit of a shrub, about the size of a
horse-chestnut ; these were strung to a piece of
bamboo, and required the individual attention of
one person to prevent them all flaring up together.

Ava was an intoxicant which all the people
indulged in ; the spirit distilled from the tee-root
was also popular ; all the chiefs possessed stills
for the production of this spirit, which was called
Lumi, resembling rum. The stems of their pipes
consisted of a hollow tube of a species of vine ;
tobacco grew in abundance.

Canoe of the Sandwich Islands with Masked Rowers

Womenfolk were not permitted too many indulgences, and under no circumstance might they eat from the same dish as the nobler sex. It would be wasting a delicacy to give them pork, or turtle, or shark, cocoanuts, bananas, or plantains, so these were *taboo* ; but they could indulge in dog's flesh, or even fish. And in 1794, a number of sheep were left in the islands of Hawaii, an arrangement having been made with the King that after their numbers had sufficiently increased the meat should not be *taboo* to the women ; but with the proviso that though the women should be allowed this food, it should not be from the identical animal partaken of by the men.

An authority on these matters says : " Notwithstanding the rigour with which these ceremonies are generally observed, the women very seldom scruple to break them " ; no doubt when there was no likelihood of their being found out. It will be hardly necessary to add that the highest in the land, the most independent—the Queen, lover of all good things, was the greatest transgressor.

The laws of marriage were very elastic, and extended to polygamy. All wives were jealously guarded against the attentions of neighbours and local residents ; but they were valuable assets to offer to visitors, when it was desirable to cement their friendship by this tie.

Women wore a simple waist cloth called *Pow*, about three yards long, and reaching below the knees ; they adorned their heads and necks with wreaths of sweet smelling leaves, purple, yellow, and white. When they swam out to the ships the dress was removed, and held by one hand out of the water to keep it dry. Men wore a small girdle made of native cloth : this girdle was called *Maro*.

In Hawaii the natives indulged in a dance, which somewhat resembled what we called ballet ; on a special occasion the ladies of the court took the principal parts. The dance space was a small square in the open, surrounded by trees and huts. The performers decked themselves in their finest array, and men their cleanest *Maros*. Women wore so many petticoats as to resemble a crinoline ; their lower limbs up to their knees were bound round with green wreaths, while their shoulders were also adorned with the broad leaves of the Tee tree. The Queen, though very anxious to take a part in these *moving pictures*, was not allowed to be present.

The wives, daughters, and sisters of the principal chief were permitted to seat themselves in the front. For music, five men beat time with a short stick on long tapering spears, each part of the spear giving a different tone ; they also sang. There were four acts to the performance, and seven performers ; as well as speaking and singing there were appropriate gestures. The principal heroine was a captive princess, and each time her name was pronounced, someone had to remove an article from her body above the waist. At the close of the last act each performer also removed some article above her waist. On other occasions men only danced in masks.

The first three acts displayed an astonishing accuracy and agility, graceful action in dancing, spirit, and vivacity. Vancouver laconically observes that " had the performance finished with the third act, we should have retired from the theatre with a much higher idea of the moral tendency of their drama, than was conveyed by the offensive libidinous scene, exhibited by the ladies in the concluding part." This *nhooarah*

A Man of the Sandwich Islands, Dancing

Facing page 76

began in the late afternoon, and lasted about an hour.

Superstition was the powerful agent by which law and order were kept ; actual punishment was very rare. In cases of theft the diviner would go through certain ceremonies, as for example burning a nut in a fire ; while it was crackling, he would say such words as " kill or shoot the fellow ; " by then the thief usually confessed. If during this awful ceremony the thief did not confess, the circumstance was reported to the King, who issued an edict throughout the island that a certain person had been robbed, and that those who were guilty had been prayed to death. The finale was, that usually the culprit pined away and died.

Their principal god was the God of Creation, called *Etooah* ; but they had seven or eight subordinate gods, represented by images of wood as ugly as sin, having their mouths all stuck round with dogs' teeth. One was sixteen feet high and three feet broad, carved out of a single tree : this god had a horrible expression, a large mouth extended with great teeth. Some were made also of stone, or a kind of wicker work covered with red feathers ; all were fearsome to look upon, and intended to excite terror.

Many of the natives believed that the first beings were descended from the gods, who were the original inhabitants of the islands. According to the priests, the first man was created by *Hanenca*, a female deity, in other words of unknown ancestry. But the most popular belief was that their ancestors came over in canoes from Tahiti. Human sacrifices were offered up on their going to war, but the usual sacrifice was pigs.

The value of a pig was estimated by its length :

a fathom pig, measured from the end of the snout to the rump was valued at two axes, a piece of sea-horse's tooth, and a fathom of European cloth. A smaller pig was measured from the elbow of one arm to the tips of the fingers when the other arm was extended.

Vancouver was privileged to take part in a solemn ceremony of consecrating the pig, but he was obliged to conform to the same customs as the natives. During the *taboo* period of two nights and one day, he had to refrain from the company of women ; partake of no food except that previously consecrated ; stay on shore and not get wetted by salt water.

The sacred rite was performed in the *Morai* at dawn of day, in the most profound silence, even that of birds and animals. The King murmured a prayer with the greatest solemnity ; in the middle of it he suddenly took up a live pig which was tied by the legs, and with one swing dashed it to death against the ground ; there must be no cry from the victim. This part of the service was a sort of introduction to the gods, after which further ceremonies took place. A large quantity of all kinds of food was then consecrated for the use of the priests and chiefs.

There was in Hawaii a peculiar connection with the number 40 ; they counted from 40 to 400, then to 4000, and afterwards to 40,000 ; every number was a fraction of 40 or 4. These people also reckoned time by the Moon.

Cook's description of the King when he came on board the *Resolution* is worthy of note : " He was of a graceful stature, about six feet high, rather corpulent, and tattooed in several parts of his body, in manner like that of other warriors. His skin was remarkably scaly ; his hair grey, and cut

King of Owyhee bringing Presents to Captain Cook.

quite short. He had very little clothing, and on his head he wore a cap of feathers."

When one of the sailors of Cook's ship died, he was interred by the natives. The grave was dug four feet deep, the bottom being covered with green leaves. A hog, roasted whole, was placed at the head and at the feet, with a quantity of plantains, bananas, and bread fruit. Finally large stones were rolled over the grave, and a stage erected over it, on which were placed more ready-cooked provisions.

At first when Captain Cook arrived with H.M.S. *Resolution* and *Adventure*, he was received with friendliness by the natives of Owhyhee (Hawaii), up to the moment of his departure; but having to return to his anchorage, owing to his being buffetted about by the winds, he met with great hostility, the people stealing every article they could lay hands on. This led to open aggression, finally ending in his death at the hands of his previous friends. It is said that Captain Cook had been impatient and severe, and had been warned by the women that his life was in danger.

Some mutilated and gnawed remains of this illustrious navigator were collected from various quarters and reverently committed to the deep; the remainder had been consumed by the warriors. It might be surprising to read that after a very drastic retaliation on the islanders by the next officer in command, he reports, "We returned to the ships before night loaded with Indian spoils . . . and having the heads of two of their fighting men stuck at the bows of the pinnaces, as a terror to the enemy."

In January, 1796, eighteen years later, H.M.S. *Providence*, with Captain Vancouver, anchored at the same bay where Captain Cook was assassinated, and was quite satisfied with his reception from the natives. He and his crew were treated with uniform goodwill and kindness. Tamaahmaah sent them ample supplies of hogs ; by this time he wore European clothes ; and on February 25th, 1794, he had ceded the Hawaiian islands to the British Empire.

HOTTENTOTS

THE country of these people is at the South end of South Africa ; they first became known to the Portuguese at the end of the 15th century, but they were not visited until about 1600, when the Dutch on their way to the East, touched at the Cape of Good Hope ; hence Boers were their first guests.

The Hottentots were at this date divided up into a number of tribes ; they were nomads, migrating from place to place, following Nature's harvests in search of food for themselves and fodder for their cattle, burning the dried-up grasses as they left. They were a trustworthy and hospitable people.

The *Khirigriquas* were one of their most numerous and powerful tribes. It was in this country that the *Cerasts*, or horned snakes, were reputed to have existed.

The origin of the Hottentots is obscure ; they declared that their first parents came in through a door or window : the man was called *Noh*, the woman *Hingnoh*.

Men had conspicuously big feet ; those of the women were, on the contrary, small and delicate. As beauty's decree had gone forth in favour of flat noses, the children had, from their infancy, their noses pressed flat. Another peculiarity of these people was, that they never cut the nails of their hands and feet.

Ancient writers declare that their *forte* was extreme laziness ; they were even too lazy to think, and it was only in urgent cases of necessity that they would help themselves. Inveterate smokers, they smoked to the point of temporarily obscuring their vision.

After a youth was initiated into manhood, he might from that time eat with his father ; he had also the privilege of being allowed to beat his mother ; and, strange though this may appear, the more violence he showed her the prouder she was of her son. The only explanation they offered for this was—that it had always been so. Another of their customs was to kill off the old people. Infanticide was also practised.

Women wore a cone-shaped hat, men a flat cap. Both were highly ornamented with any odds and ends such as buttons or saucer-shaped medallians, or strings of beads ; a mirror was a much prized possession. Men carried, suspended from the neck, a small bag or purse, containing a knife, pipe, tobacco, and a *Daccha*—a small stick burnt at both ends, which they used as a talisman. These little bags were sometimes made out of an old glove obtained from a European. Women carried a similar bag, but it was larger and hung from the waist.

Men, women, and children were slaves to the habit of smearing their bodies with butter or mutton fat mixed with ashes ; this compound was removed as soon as it became dry. The nobility of anyone depended entirely on the quality of the butter or fat used—hence they ranked according to smell ; yet for all their love of oil, they had a horror of fish oil.

Although mentally lazy the Hottentots were remarkable for their fleetness in running ; they had also a great reputation as hunters. Packs of them would run down a lion, rhinoceros, or elephant, and after surrounding the animal they speared it to death. The honour conferred on successful hunters, was associated with very revolting details connected with the filthy ingredients and garbage, with which they were smeared.

These people lived in *kraals* ranging from four to five hundred inhabitants in each ; the roofs of the huts were so low that it was not possible to stand, so everyone squatted ; and there being no other outlet for the smoke of the fire to escape, it came out through the door. To both sexes the eating of pork and fish without scales was *taboo* ; as also among men, not women, was the eating of rabbits or hares. A beast's entrails, partly boiled in its own blood, to which was added some milk, they considered their most dainty dish.

Hottentots were excessively dirty and covered by lice of extraordinary dimensions. Since, they said, these parasites live on us, why should we not, as an act of reciprocity, feed on them ? During hard times they boiled down the discarded skin shoes of the Europeans and, according to their tastes, enjoyed the meal this afforded them.

In their dances the musical accessories were a one-string bow with a quill attachment through which the performer blew. Women's fingers were used in the place of drum sticks, while there were the usual cries of encouragement from the women who formed the orchestra.

A circle was formed solely of men, who joined hands. Inside this circle only one couple took part. Facing each other, and wide apart, they commenced stamping with their characteristic motion, at the same time gradually drawing nearer one another. When they finally met this dance ended ; and another couple were allowed into the circle until every one had had a turn.

Marriages were arranged by the parents : should the girl take a dislike to her future selected partner, there was still one way of escape open to her ; for if she was successful in resisting his seductions, in spite of being obliged to remain in his company until the following morning, she was free from the bargain. Marriage between cousins was prohibited, the penalty for this offence being death. In spite of their love for their own music, it was never heard at their marriage festivities, but after the company had feasted, a pipe was lit, and handed round, each one taking a few whiffs.

If a widow re-married she had the joint of her little finger cut off, and every time she re-married she lost another joint. The birth of male twins was a source of great rejoicing ; if they were twin girls they were destroyed ; if a boy and girl, the latter was placed on the branch of a tree and left there to perish. If a child was still-born it was regarded as a most evil omen and the parents hastily moved their hut.

When the woman had recovered she daubed herself with cow-dung, which was considered a form of purification and, as Lady Augusta Hamilton tells us, after " being thus delightfully perfumed, and elegantly decorated with sheep's guts," she was permitted once more to visit and receive company.

The Hottentots kept a sort of fighting bull ; these would, like sheep-dogs when there were signs of a stranger, call in all the cattle and drive them into the *kraal*. They acted also the part of watch-dogs, and woe betide a strolling stranger should he fail in treating them with respect.

Every family manufactured its own pottery, made of a clay obtained from the material of which ants' nests were made ; when mixed with ants' eggs it formed a paste ; the ware was then shaped by hands and baked in a hole in a forest. Sewing needles they made from the quill of a bird's wing ;

thread was obtained from the small nerves of animals.

During the Dutch occupation, in the middle of the 17th century, the usual mode of measuring out a new farm was to pace the ground ; half an hour's striding in each direction from the position of the homestead was the regulated extent of the farm. After a lapse of a century and a half, the Europeans acquired possession of nearly the whole region inhabited by the Hottentots.

The essence of these people's religion was their implicit faith in their traditional customs ; it became an instinct to preserve them. There was also a great fear of consequences from their neglect. They apparently believed that this instinctive feeling remained active after death, and that this spirit jealously watched over its rites among the living, both for the welfare of the individual as well as for the community.

When many inhabitants were stricken by death, the cause was attributed to some salutary message from the spirits of the dead to mend their ways. The witch doctor was probably the reasoning brain of the tribe, and could trace the source of pollution : the *kraal* was moved elsewhere ; the sacrifice of an animal or a slave was necessary as a means of maintaining friendship with the guardian spirits. A portion of the feast was then consumed by the people, the remainder went to the witch doctor, while the share of the guardian spirits was the spiritual food suggested by the slaughtered animal.

There was some form of court of justice to decide disputes ; the verdict depended entirely on the majority of supporters on either side. In fact all the inhabitants formed themselves into a jury. In serious criminal cases the sentences night be

banishment from the *kraal* ; in this case the culprit
vanished into the bush and was seen no more,
being an outcast from all other *kraals*.   Possibly
capital punishment might be inflicted on the
offender ; when this occurred it was considered that
he had sufficiently atoned for the crime, and his
family also were forgiven.   All property was
inherited by the eldest son ; it was never divided,
neither did any woman inherit.

There was a certain kind of flying two-horned
beetle, for which these people had a kind of
veneration ; it was about the size of a small
child's finger, had a green back, and was speckled
underneath red and white.   When one of these
beetles was seen, all gathered round it and addressed
it in endearing terms as a special symbol of
heaven.

The Hottentots had a belief in a Creative God
called *Gounja*—that is, God of Gods, but they had
no forms or ceremonies connected with worship.
To their idea, he was simply a great and good man
in whom all trust could be placed.   His abode was,
they believed, a long way beyond the Moon.   They
reverenced the Moon, and offered sacrifices in
honour of each new phase, praying to it for weather
favourable to the pastures.   The Moon was, in
fact, the visible symbol of the greater and invisible
spirit.

These Hottentot people are now nearly extinct.

JAVA

JAVA is an island in the Eastern Archipelago. The Javanese claim a Chinese origin, and physically there is a strong likeness between the two nations. Marco Polo, who lived many years among the Tartars, heard from them that Java paid them regularly a yearly tribute.

The Javanese were an essentially ease-loving nation, and work did not greatly appeal to them. They had also an immense sense of their own importance, and never permitted an equal to sit an inch higher than themselves. The king was an absolute autocrat, dealing out life and death as it pleased him. For every murder committed he was paid a fine, hence crime was remarkably remunerative to his majesty, more especially as the relations of the murdered man usually kept up the feud and tried to kill the murderer or his relatives : if they succeeded, further fines were naturally forthcoming. The usual weapon they carried was called *criss*, a sharp and very edged knife about two feet long. These weapons had handles of wood or horn, curiously carved in the shape of a devil ; these handles were worshipped by many of the people.

A Javanese might have three wives, and for each wife he was obliged to keep ten female slaves ; he could indeed have as many more as he pleased, and use them as concubines. Many of the better class spent their days sitting cross-legged, cutting and carving sticks, which they did remarkably well. They were great eaters, although their slaves were given nothing more palatable than herbs and roots, and rice soaked in water.

The toilette of the élite consisted of a loin cloth
of fine painted calico, and a *tuke*, or turban on
their heads.　On rare and very special occasions
they wore a close-fitting coat of cloth, velvet or
silk.　The lower orders wrapped round their waists
a kind of girdle of calico, which had always to be
at least a yard wide ; if they covered their heads
it was with a flat velvet cap, but having fine heads
of curly hair, they for the most part preferred to
show it.　The women were all bareheaded, but
the better classes tucked theirs up in a fashion of
their own ; they wore the same kind of loin cloths
of painted calico, and were most particular to
have a piece of the same material over their
shoulders, with the ends hanging down.

Most of the Javanese were very religious,
although they seldom went to church.　Some of
them were Mahometans, but many believed in
Naby Isa or the Prophet Jesus.　The poorer
orders had little knowledge of any religion, but
believed that God had created the world and
everything in it, and that he meant well by them ;
whereas with a philosophy which had much to
commend it, they felt it more prudent to propitiate
the devil, who certainly did not mean well by
them, and who would most assuredly do his best
to injure them.

After the Spaniards were established in Malaya,
the customs of the Javanese somewhat changed.
Among the many petty chieftains in the island,
those of *Bantam* had always been the most powerful ; but the most beautiful town was *Tuban*,
where all the commerce from Holland was established.　Here the Dutch kept high court, and lived
as princes ; here, too, special elephants were kept
for the mutilation and slaughter of culprits ; these
elephants were also taught to wield a weapon

held by their trunks, and thus were used as soldiers.

Every conceivable article of clothing was procurable at *Bantam* : one quarter of the town was set apart for men's apparel, another for that of women ; in this quarter no man was permitted to enter. At this town there were ten women to one man, hence concubinage naturally flourished. Their offspring were, however, considered legitimate although they were frequently poisoned. The king, as will be seen in Sumatra, usually took possession of female children after the death of their fathers ; in order to frustrate this, girls were often married before they reached the age of eight.

Women of the higher class were very carefully guarded ; a son, after he had reached manhood, was not permitted to enter his mother's apartment. Women seldom went out ; when they did, any man they met, except the king, was obliged to hide until they had passed. Every man of rank always walked about in state followed by his servants : one carried the umbrella over his master's head, another the box of betel which he chewed at intervals. Betel is the leaf of a creeper —chewed with it is the *areca* nut from the palm tree. A little packet is made with the leaf as an envelope, and contains a portion of nut and a pinch of quicklime ; this mixture is put into the mouth and chewed. So strong a hold had this habit over the women also, that they kept a packet of betel near their beds to chew during the night , they also kept a slave to perform the elegant duty of scratching their backs.

Among their strange customs was that, if a house caught fire, it was the work of women to extinguish it ; the sole part that men played in the disaster was to stand on guard armed, lest any robbery was committed. If during a quarrel a man killed his adversary, dreading the punishment which might await him, he promptly proceeded to run amok, killing right and left ; not even children were spared as he darted away in desperation. We hear that he was very seldom taken alive.

So suspicious were these people of one another that they slept with their *criss* under their pillow. A brother would not even receive his brother without having his *criss* handy, not to mention three or four throwing knives ; in regard to their trading they were equally suspicious and crafty. These people were extremely ingenious. They wrote on leaves of a particular kind of tree, with a sharp pointed instrument ; these leaves, placed between pieces of wood, thus formed a book.

The most popular pastime among the Javanese, indeed one common to all the Malay races, was cock fighting. In Java they even held fighting matches between quails ; for these combats the male was considered too small and timid, so they made use of the more irascible hen birds, and often hazarded considerable sums on the result. The sport of kite flying also enthralled them ; the object of each player in this game being to break the string of his adversary's kite. In any small town it was no uncommon sight to see fifty or sixty paper kites being guided against each other.

A traveller in the latter part of the tenth century affirms that combats between wild beasts were arranged for the amusement of the Javanese, those between the tiger and buffalo being the most popular, each animal having been previously excited or irritated to its utmost fury.

At about this same period it is related that criminals who had been condemned to death were pitted against tigers. The unfortunate men were clothed in a sort of yellow jacket and armed with the native *criss*. Stavorinus relates a singular circumstance which befell a criminal condemned to be devoured by tigers : When he was thrown into a ditch in which were the tigers, he fell astride upon the back of the largest of these. The animal exhibited so much astonishment and alarm that he made no attempt to injure the man, and none of the others dared attack him in such a situation. This incident did not, however, save the poor fellow's life, for the ruthless prince gave orders that he should be killed.

In 1912 two men were thrown to wild beasts by order of the Sultan ; each was armed with a *criss*, the point of which had been blunted. One of the criminals was immediately torn to pieces, but the other maintained the fight for nearly two hours, and finally succeeded in killing the tiger.

MALAYA

THE Malayan Archipelago comprises a group of islands, the largest being Sumatra, Borneo, Java, Celebes and the Philippine Islands ; the Malayan race, moreover, extends over the northern side of New Guinea. Only, however, the inhabitants of the Malay Peninsula, that portion of mainland lying to the south of Siam, will be dealt with. Singapore lies at the extreme south end of the Peninsula.

Whatever may have been the origin, the name Malaya implies something superior. The inhabitants were partially Mahometans, but they were not devout by nature and hankered after what their Moslem law strictly forbade in regard to witchcraft ; while mixed with this religion was a strong element of their ancient paganism.

There were, seemingly, no customs or marriage laws, no barriers to intrigues. The primary public policy was the increase of the population ; special officials were told off to beat a drum from darkness to dawn, for the purpose of instilling into those of a ripe age the desire to fulfil their marital duties.

The women, like most women, loved jewellery, and delighted to decorate themselves with bracelets, earrings, and necklets of diamonds and rubies, as well as all kinds of pearls. These were easily procurable for the better classes ; but as there was no coin currency riches were measured by nutmeg property. Malaya was the only country, except a few surrounding islands, in which nutmegs grew. The women were obliged sadly to use their precious ornaments as a means of barter. Men exhibited their vanity by perfuming themselves

with sweet-scented oils ; both sexes had large
eyes with very long lashes, which they accentuated
by the use of dark pigments.

The characteristics of these people sound the
reverse of attractive, for they are described as
being suspicious, untrustworthy and totally lacking
in gratitude.

Ternate is the chief island of the group ; in it
were a large number of albinos, but there were
very few men of that description. Apart from
this physical peculiarity a malformed person was
unknown ; all the inhabitants were, on the
contrary, symmetrical and well-formed.

A very ancient form of veil was worn by the
women, which hung from the forehead in six
strips, completely covering the face ; it is claimed
that this form of headdress descended to them from
the times of Abraham. Among other treasures
greatly prized was a two-headed snake of gold,
said to be of very ancient origin.

Propitiation of demons kept these people exceedingly busy, as well as causing them much uneasiness.
When starting on a journey, should either a funeral
be the first object they met, or the scream of a
night-bird be heard, or a crow fly over their heads,
it might be taken for certain that misfortune
loomed in the near future ; to prevent which,
necessitated a return to their homes. Another of
their superstitions was that they could never be
induced to sell any fish caught in a new net,
although they might eat it themselves or give it
away. Girls were not allowed to eat a certain
very luscious fig, nor any double fruit, lest they
gave birth to twins. And if a woman died in
childbirth, or when she was *enceinte*, it was believed
that she would be changed into a kind of demon.

Another of their curious beliefs was, that in the

hair lay unseen forces which would sustain them
under the most grievous trials, and give them
courage to confess any crime they had committed.
Consequently, having their hair shaved was the
greatest possible disaster, as it entirely deprived
them of this mental strength. The people kept
professional necromancers ; women usually, of
course, consulted them in regard to their amours.
These sorcerers had a great reputation, more
especially in the preparation of poisons.

As late as 1854 it was a rule at *Lomback* that
anyone found in a house after dark was liable to
be stabbed and his body thrown into the street.
Laws were exceedingly drastic in regard to breaking
the marriage contract : a married woman might
not even receive a cigarette from a stranger under
penalty of death. More serious infidelity was
punished by the woman and her paramour being
tied back to back and thrown into the sea.

In *Amboyna,* as soon as a child was born it was
given a birth name, independently of what it
would afterwards be called ; this birth name was
invariably associated with some circumstance connected with the moment of birth. Children were
always carried on the hip. A son inherited all
his deceased father's goods, and only allowed his
mother and sisters sufficient for their subsistence.
Any title the father happened to possess went to
a collateral relation.

The inland natives, those who lived in the mountains, were of a much larger build than those on
the coast or near rivers. They were also more
vigorous and barbaric, and most of both sexes
went about nude. They interlaced the shell of a
cocoa-nut into their hair, at the top of their heads,
and surrounded it with white shells ; these same
white shells they used as necklets, and on the

toes of each foot. They also wore very large
yellow ear-rings, and they never dressed without
a branch of evergreen twisted round their arms
and knees.

Among these mountaineers, it was an inviolable
law that no young man was allowed to cover his
nakedness, nor put a roof on his house, nor marry,
nor do any work. On each occasion of any special
undertakings he brought a human head to the
village ; this offering was placed on a stone consecrated for that purpose. The degree of nobility
of a man depended upon the number of heads
taken. In " head hunting " the young men went
in groups of eight or ten ; each was camouflaged
by green branches and moss ; and so well disguised, that they were indistinguishable from the
forest growth. These gallants waited for any
passer-by, and after killing him and cutting off his
head, they made a solemn entry into the village,
where the young females shouted with triumph
and exultation, dancing round the braves, and an
orgy of rioting ensued. Later the heads were left
hanging from the houses. Occasionally one of the
braves had the peculiarly unpleasing experience of
having his own head chopped off ; in this case his
body was thrown into a bush as being unfit for
decent burial.

Most of their wars were caused by some imagined
insult to their dignity. For example, when visiting a neighbour, tobacco and *pisang* (a form of
betel nut) would be offered ; should, however, the
host either purposely or by accident omit to offer
the leaves necessary for chewing the *pisang*—then
the trouble began. The insult could only be
condoned by a suitable present ; otherwise, it
became a case of a family feud which might
continue through many generations.

Again, should any child of the host blow his
nose, it was regarded as an outrage ; if the host's
children threw something at a stranger, or laughed
at him, a present must be made to atone for such
outrageous behaviour. If the father refused compensation, possibly some two or three years later
the insulted party would return for satisfaction.
Should the offender die in the meanwhile, his
offence would be passed on to his descendants.
Sometimes the whole village sided with the
aggrieved party (although in the meantime he
may have actually died), and retaliated by taking
the heads of the aggressor's villagers, without the
smallest connection with the injured.

When starting for war, should the occasion
demand such an extreme step, they called upon
the heavens, the earth, sea, and rivers, as well as
all their ancestors to aid them ; then, turning
towards the enemy, they told them that they
would not attack them clandestinely, like robbers,
but give them fair warning.

These same mountaineers of Amboyna ate
snakes, rats, and frogs ; they also made a fermented drink from sago. But, being cannibals,
their most dainty food was human flesh. An old
king named Titaway, in 1687, confessed that in
his time he had eaten many of his enemies, but
that they had first been roasted. He admitted
that among all sorts of meat none was so delicate
as the human body, more particularly the cheeks
and hands. And Mr. Henry Hawke, evidently
alluding to cannibalism, says quaintly, " I have
seen the bones of a Spaniard that have been so
clean burnished, as though it had been done by
men that had no other occupation."

MARIANNE ISLANDS (LADRONES)

THE *Marianne* islands were also discovered in 1521 by Magellan, but were later on re-named in honour of Marie-Anne of Austria, Queen of Spain, when taken possession of in 1565. Although only about 900 miles from the Philippines, the personal characteristics of the inhabitants more resembled a mixture of Japanese and the aborigines of the Philippines, known as *Tagales*. The principal island of the group was Guaham. Before the advent of the Spaniards the natives lived an absolutely natural life, untrammelled by any laws except their few customs. They were unaware of any other lands, and thought themselves the only people in existence. De la Harpe shrewdly observes that they were entirely without the many things which we consider necessary for existence, and which of course it was thought expedient to thrust on them for the sake of trade.

Their only bird was a species of dove, which they tamed and taught to speak. It is related as an astounding fact that until 1566 they had never seen fire ; their first introduction to it being the burning of one of their houses on the occasion of Magellan's visit. At first they thought it was a kind of animal which attached itself to and ate up wood. So greatly were they in fear of it that they would never approach a fire, which, as they said, by its very breath made their bodies sore. However, they very soon learnt to master and apply it.

When the Jesuits first visited these islands they were densely populated. The inhabitants are described as a peaceful people of remarkably fine physique, free of disease, and living to a very old age. The necessities of their life were but few, and their additional wants easily satisfied. It was this contentment, this want of ambition for anything more, that gave the missionaries so much trouble ; the people were simply not interested in anything beyond what they already possessed.

At their gatherings they feasted off fish, fruits, and roots, drinking a liquid made from rice and cocoa-nut. At their dances they always recounted the deeds of their ancestors. Women decorated themselves with shells threaded with very fine roots, pieces of tortoiseshell hung from their necks, flowers were intertwined in their hair ; and, it is related, that whatever decorations and leaves they hung about them, rather disfigured than ornamented their figures. Musical sounds were produced by using shells as castanets, and doubtless their soft and cooing voices, combined with their suggestive gestures, made them most alluring to the onlookers. Men were completely nude, shaved of all hair with the exception of a little tuft, about three inches long, on the top of their heads. Beauty and adornment in women were represented by black teeth, and long hair which was whitened by lime. Yet with all their simplicity they reverted very strongly to class distinction. As is the case in every land, some asserted themselves so much above the others that they became tyrannical in the extreme ; so select, indeed, did they become, that they considered it a crime to associate with, or marry into, the " lower " classes ; even in regard to speech, the plebeian ones were obliged to make their requests from a distance. But the rarer blossoms were extremely courteous when addressing each other (typical of the Japanese) ; when meeting, the salutation consisted of affectionately patting each other on the stomach.

When a man died his children did not succeed,

but his brother, or his sister's son ; the argument being that no man could be certain whether the children of his wife were also his, whereas the children of his sister must be hers, and consequently came of the same stock as himself : this custom ensured the property being kept in the family. Almost from their infancy, children were quite independent of their parents.

These people were extraordinarily expert with their light canoes. The only arms they possessed was a club, made of the arm and leg-bone of a man, with a pointed end, and so sharp that the slightest stab would kill. They were also such experts at stone throwing that they could almost penetrate through trees. Men never forgave or forgot an insult, although a long time might elapse before they took revenge. Homicide and theft were regarded with the greatest abhorrence ; houses could therefore be left open with perfect safety and nothing out of them would ever be missing.

But there was a fly in the ointment of this gentle people which became visible in regard to their marriage customs. A man might take as many wives as he chose, but he usually found that one was sufficient. This commendable abnegation was not so surprising, when one learns that women were so much mistress in their own houses that a man was not even allowed to touch anything without obtaining her permission. If he lost his temper, or did any of the things he ought not to do, the woman either chastised or left him, taking her children and her chattels with her ; thus at any moment a man could be left by a capricious woman. For her, all became once more serene when she and the children adopted another man. If a man's wife had a liaison, his only remedy was separation ; he had no right to punish his rival.

Should, on the other hand, a man have an *affaire*, his wife called upon all the women she could muster ; each armed herself with a stick, and put on her husband's hat. Thus they advanced towards the habitation of the guilty husband, tore up his crops, treading them under foot ; and having broken everything they could lay their hands upon, they finally beat him and drove him away. He might, indeed, consider himself lucky if, in addition to this ill-treatment, they did not pillage everything he possessed and destroy his dwelling. This drastic system of dealing with man's frailties was hardly calculated to produce in young men a yearning to marry ; they found considerably less discomfort in hiring girls, or buying them from their parents for a piece of iron or tortoise-shell. These girls were kept in a separate establishment, which their lovers visited when they desi:ed.

It was in these islands that Dampier first discovered the bread-fruit tree. He describes the fruit as being the size of a man's head ; when cooked it tasted like our white bread with a flavour of banana, and was very nourishing.

There were no animals whatever in these islands, not even a mouse ; the only animal food was a kind of wild-fowl. But Nature had in all respects released these people from any struggle for existence. Time in their lives had no meaning, for beyond the division of a day into an almost equal night, each day monotonously succeeded another ; while the season's clock of ripening fruits, was merely the procession of pleasant occurrences, and taken as a matter of course.

Very few people could be more eloquent in their bereavements, or more lugubrious in their wailings at a death : they wept, literally, in torrents. Their cries were heart-rending ; they also abstained, at least for seven or eight days, from all kinds of food, during which period they kept up a doleful dirge. On a necklet or a cord a knot was tied on each anniversary of a lost child or parent. The wails of tribulation were devastating in the case of the death of a woman belonging to the exclusive class. Trees were uprooted, houses burned, canoes destroyed ; paths were strewn with fresh palm branches ; while one and all lifted up their voices in some extravagant and poetical rhapsody regarding his affliction, such as, " There is no more life for me now " ; " The Sun which animated me is eclipsed " ; " The Moon which illuminated my way is obscured " ; " The Star which guided me is extinguished."

These people had great belief in the power of their magicians to control the elements, produce rain or sunshine, as well as to cure diseases and bring success in all their undertakings. They had also, apparently, some vague ideas of a Devil somewhere, in a place where he could torment them—and of a Paradise ; but their future destiny in either place did not seem to depend so much upon their manner of life as on their manner of death. Those who died a violent death would find themselves in a place inhabited by the Devil ; but those who died a natural death would eat of the fruits of Paradise, where sugar-cane and cocoanuts were even more delicious than on earth.

MARQUESAS ISLANDS

THESE islands were discovered by the Spaniards in 1795 and named after the Marquess of Mendana, viceroy of Peru, under whose protection the expedition started. *Nikerheva* is the principal island of the group ; and the inhabitants of the Typee (Taipi) valley are the most noteworthy. It is recorded that cannibalism was prevalent in all these islands, the menu consisting of slain enemies only ; and as Typee signifies eaters of human flesh, it is possible that this particular tribe were specially addicted to this gruesome form of repast : they have undoubtedly been credited with murdering and eating all the crew of a vessel which visited those waters.

They are a brown, coffee-coloured race with straight hair, but as in Tahiti, the natives yearned after fairness of skin. The juice of the *popa* root was much resorted to as a cosmetic for this purpose, and in addition to acquiring what nature had denied, they screened themselves, when possible, from the direct sun rays. Five or six times a day they bathed, drying their luxurious hair after each time of bathing, then washed it in fresh water, finally perfuming it with a powerfully scented oil made from the cocoa-nut.

The distinctive characteristics of these islands is the European caste of features ; and all voyagers call attention to the symmetrical and physical beauty of the Typees ; their dress was merely a minimum covering, easily put on, easier removed.

Russell, in his *Polynesia*, tells us how they excelled in tattooing, though very young girls had few of these ornamentations ; but as they grew older they had their right hand and left foot most

elaborately tattooed ; this was also an indication
that they were married. Among men who had
reached very mature age this tattooing had been
so frequent, that according to Herman Melville
they occasionally presented the most repulsive
appearance, their skin covered by deep indentations
and fissures. By long practice of this custom their
bodies sometimes became a dull green hue ; in
addition their heads were quite bald, while their
feet were unlike any ordinary feet, their toes
standing out in every direction. The reason of
this does not seem very clear, it may possibly have
been due to their constant use as fingers.

The principal food of the Typees was one of
the many preparations from the bread-fruit tree.
This fruit is the size of a citron melon, and after
the rind has been removed resembles white pulp ;
the leaves are of enormous size, scalloped at the
edge. When nearing the stage of decay their
colour becomes of a many-hued richness, and the
natives wore them as strikingly picturesque head-
dresses. The Typee maidens delighted in flowers,
and not being less vain than most maidens, they
wore dainty single hybiscus in their ears, and
necklaces, coronets, bracelets, etc., of intertwined
leaves and blossoms.

They were magnificent swimmers—even infants
of a few days old were taught to swim—so had
no use for canoes, which were *taboo* for women and
would have meant instant death.

A favourite drink in the South Sea Islands was
called *arva*, made from a root, in much the same
fashion as *kava* was made in Tonga : its primary
effect was stimulating, then it acted more as a
narcotic. But in the Typee valley it was usually
drunk at their convivial gatherings as an ordinary
stimulant. Their music must have suggested

something weird, for besides drums they had nasal flutes, which were blown through the left nostril, the other being closed by a muscular contraction.

In regard to their marriages, a man might have but one wife, while a girl was allowed at least two husbands—probably because the males far outnumbered the females—yet any form of marriage was usually dispensed with. The girls were wooed at a very early age, and when, as frequently occurred, they tired of one another, a third party in the shape of a man swooped down and carried them off to his hut ; it would seem this *ménage à trois* worked very harmoniously.

We hear of a curious observance which was practised every night. The inmates of a house, as they sat on their mats, would commence a low dismal chant—not song—with music made by two small sticks tapped slowly together, and held by each person present for an hour or two. Whether it was a religious rite or merely to induce sleep is not known.

The religious rites of fanaticism and horror were held in the *Hoolah Hoolah* ground in the *taboo* groves of the valley. At each end of this spot was a high terraced altar, guarded by a multitude of frightful idols. Gigantic trees stood in the centre, with huge and gradually spreading trunks railed in with sugar canes, from which the priests declaimed thair pagan teachings. The fear of *taboo* guarded the secrets of their sacrificial rites : should any female enter or even touch with her feet this sacred ground, she was immediately killed.

Apart from the rites held in the *Hoolah Hoolah* ground, the Typees held funeral orgies from which all sense of decency was omitted : dancing, singing and feasting lasting for two days after the burial. They had mastered either the art of embalming

or "fuming"; the bodies were hung up on the
side of the house close by the skulls of their
enemies killed in battle.

During the past half a century, the number of
these classic people are dwindling to extinction;
the debased remnant have lost all affinity with
the unique environment of the beautiful valley
of Typee.

THE NETHERLANDS

THE Dutch were described in 1760 as being tall and strongly built, but in his *Geographical and Historical Grammar*, Mr. Salmon says, " both Men and Women have the grossest Shapes that are to be met with anywhere, or rather no Shape at all. Nor is their Motion less disagreeable than their Shape ; they move heavily and awkwardly." He is kinder to their features and complexions, and allows the Boors or Husbandmen are industrious, "but slow of understanding ; not to be dealt with by hasty Words, but easily manag'd by soft and fair, and yielding to plain Reason if you give them Time to understand it."

The seamen were, apparently, a mannerless crew "which is usually mistaken for Pride." Sir William Temple accounts for their surliness, "from their conversing with Winds and Waves that are not to be wrought upon by Language."

The dress of these people, with the exception of the officers of the Army, seems to lack entirely in elegance : "Their Coats have neither Shape nor Pleats, and their long Pockets are set as high as their Ribs ; but that of the Women appear something odd to us, their Coats coming no lower than the Middle of their Legs."

Their many taxes included a Land-tax, Poll-tax and Hearth-tax. The amusements of the Hollanders were varied, but "they seldom play for any Thing but Drink, and the Tavern where they spend their Winnings always concludes the Diversions of the Day. *Hans* never cares to go to Bed without his Dose." They seem to have been a stolid people ; quarrels were rare, revenge still rarer, while the sensation of jealousy was almost

unknown : " Their Tempers are not airy enough
for Joy, nor any unusual Strains of pleasant
Humour, nor warm enough for Love. . . . The
Men are addicted to Drinking, which some think
necessary in this Foggy Air, for their Health as
well as the Improvement of their Understandings."

The inhabitants of Holland may be divided into
the following classes : The *Peasants* or *Boors*, who
cultivated the land ; the *Marriners* or *Schippers*,
who supplied their ships with produce ; the
Merchants or *Traders*, who filled their towns for
the purpose of Barter ; the *Renteeners*, or Men
who lived in the principal cities upon their Rents,
or interests of Estates previously acquired by
their families ; Lastly, the Gentlemen and Officers
of their Princes.

As an example of their hospitality, the following
was written by an English gentleman (1691),
attending the Court of the King of Great Britain
after a voyage to Holland : " When you are
entered in the house; the first thing you encounter
is a Looking-Glass ; no question but a true
Embleme of Politick Hospitality ; for though it
reflect your selfe in your own Figure, 'tis yet no
longer than while you are there before it. When
you are gone once, it Flatters the next Comer,
without the least remembrance that you e'er were
there."

A custom regarding the period of childbirth,
suggests both thoughtfulness and philosophy and
is thus described : " When the Woman lies in,
the Ringle of the door does penance, and is lapped
about with Linen, either to show you that loud
knocking may wake the Child, or else that for
a month the Ring is not to be run at. But if
the Child be dead, there is thrust out a Nosegay
tied to a stick's end ; perhaps for an Emblem of

the Life of Man, which may wither as soon as born ; or else to let you know that though these fade upon their gathering, yet from the same stock the next year a new shoot may spring."

A French voyager in the Pays-bas Unis (1815), tells us that the Dutch believed in a numerous progeny which indeed outnumbered any other country in Europe. The customs in regard to their period of engagement differed in every town and village. Among the bourgeois classes, the fiancée sent round to all her relations and friends some *hypocras* or wine, in which cinnamon, bark, and sugar were infused in bottles ornamented with true lovers' knots in ribbon, symbolizing " fiancée's tears."

Women multiplied plentifully, as we have heard. Immediately their first child was born, the father announced the tidings to all friends and relations. In *Haarlem* and *Enkhuisen* there was attached to all the doors where a woman was lying-in, a small board covered with rose-coloured silk, above which was a piece of lace folded in the shape of a fan. This board was never removed until the mother was able to rise from her bed ; during the time it was there no creditors nor officers of justice were allowed to disturb the husband, be the pretext what it might.

A curious sight might sometimes be seen in the streets ; children dressed half in black and half in white, with chamois leather gloves up to their elbows. These were orphans, and their bizarre appearance was to call attention to their existence, and to move the heart of the generous. One might also see a number of lugubrious faced men in sombre black clothes with a white cravat, a long trailing crêpe hat-band, an umbrella under the arm, a cigar in the mouth, with pencil and mourning cards, who ringing at the door-bell would bear the invitations of the obsequies of those who were no more.

The houses were built of light material, with a central room to which no sunlight ever penetrated, but was protected from the cold by being surrounded by other rooms : this was the family's sitting apartment. The staircase had the steepness of ladders or of ships' gangways. On entering a working man's house a few articles of furniture were seen scattered about the receiving room, but where were the beds ?—behind a cupboard or door, let into the wall, one above the other.

The mention of Holland was associated with the *Kermesses* or Fair. Teniers has popularized them in his pictures but not idealized them. These outbursts remained for long the passion of the people ; they are described as the unleashing of the human heart of primitive humanity. They took place both in towns as well as in country districts. Men who at one moment were respectable citizens suddenly became frolicsome and irresponsible. A crowd might be looking at some illumination, when suddenly the old cry, " Hos, Hos," would be started. This refrain acted like magic ; a sort of frenzy ensued, the people joining arms, commencing to jump, stamping their sabots, and jostling their neighbours. Everyone indeed was in a state of delirium, and not a few were given up to complete sottishness.

These *Kermesses* were not the Hollanders' only form of delirium ; for travellers in the 16th century wondered more than a little at the wild excitement in which the whole of the population behaved during the skating season, when the inland waters became solid enough to support them.

They had other channels in which they displayed
an unconscious sense of humour. If a man kissed
a girl without her sanction, she complained to the
Burgomaster. The matter was seriously referred
to the Tribunal at Utrecht ; from here it was
passed on to the Court of Appeal at Amsterdam,
who were indulgent enough to exonerate the
criminal—because a kiss was a justifiable expression of admiration, and moreover such a motive
was not criminal.

At *Gouda* is to be found the long "church-
warden" pipe, which the bridegroom smoked on
the eve of his marriage ; and to show his capability
in smoking and handling the pipe, he laid it back
without breaking the old clay stem. This pipe
was the emblem of the husband's dignity ; it also
indicated that in the house he was lord and master.
Smoking was a national trait ; frequently a child
of eight might be met, walking between his parents
and smoking a cigar.

In this land were water and fire vendors ; and
in the early hours servants were sent out to buy
a quantity of boiling water for breakfast, or some
hot embers for lighting a fire.

Among their superstitions Monday was considered an unlucky day to commence a journey.

A traveller to Holland early in the 19th century,
remarked on the over scrupulous neatness and
cleanliness of the people of *Broek* ; the paving of
the main street was of fine polished stones and
bricks of various colours, resembling a mosaic,
and kept spotlessly clean and polished. The
houses were like dolls' houses, looking as if they
had just come from the toy makers ; each painted
in various bright colours with pavements of various
coloured stones, resembling the contours of flowers
and streets, and everything, everywhere, carefully

washed and polished every day. But to keep
their houses so spotless, at the threshold of the
house, the visitor was expected to exchange his
boots for a pair of slippers.

Cows were regularly stabled, curried and rubbed
down ; the tails of the cows were all turned up
and secured to the rafters of the roof. But the
strangest custom of all, thought this traveller,
was that they never opened the principal apartment of their house except at the baptism, the
marriage, or the death of any member of the
family. At other times it was hermetically closed
and kept sacred.

At Amsterdam, criminals whose offences were
not capital were placed in the *Rasphuis*; their
employment consisted of sawing wood. If they
were indolent or refractory they were shut up in
a cellar into which water was allowed to run ; so
unless they worked at a pump which was fixed
there, they must be drowned.

The *Spinhuis* was another singular establishment. In this building one part was devoted to
women whose offences were not of an aggravated
character, and another separate part for serious
offences. Young ladies of even high families were
sometimes sent to the former place, on account of
undutiful behaviour or domestic offences. They
were compelled to wear a distinctive dress and
work a certain number of hours a day. Husbands
who had to complain of the extravagance of their
wives could send them to the *Spinhuis* to acquire
more sober " habits " ; on the other hand, a wife
who brought a complaint against her husband
might have him accommodated with lodgings in
this charitable Institution.

NORTH AMERICAN INDIANS

THE original stock of these people was presumably an overflow of Asiatics by way of the Behring Straits. When Europeans first became acquainted with these Indians, they had spread, fan-like, and occupied an area extending about 1500 miles north and south, and 2000 miles across the North American Continent. They were located on both sides of the Rocky Mountains.

The most Northerly groups were the *Blood Indians*, *Crees*, while the *Camanchees* and *Norahoes* were on the borders of Mexico. The renowned *Sioux Indians* occupied the central area.

In appearance they were all fundamentally alike, usually of a dark copper colour, with very long black hair, especially the men. When first known, they numbered about sixteen millions, but in 1833 they were reduced to less than two millions. To use their own figure of speech, " We are travelling to the Shades of our fathers, towards the setting Sun." All these people erected tents of hide, called *Tipis* ; all dressed in the skins of animals, and all vied with one another in the gaudinesss of their apparel, and decorations of porcupine quills and birds' feathers, especially those of the eagle.

The custom of scalping was universal ; when a man was killed in combat, or trapped in their perpetual raids, the victor would cut about four inches off the skin of his enemy's head, with the hair attached—a deed of which the victor was mightily proud. The scalp having proclaimed him to be a warrior, it was then dried, and finally secured to the end of a spear, or to a war club ; it might even be stitched to his clothing as an ornament, and became ever after an honoured trophy, and an evidence of distinction. It was also honoured by a public orgy and dance, after which it was returned to its owner.

Another universal object of pride among the Indians was their pipe ; not only was it an emblem of dignity but of utility, being from 4 to 5 feet long, and decorated in various colours ; the bowl part was made out of a special red stone, said to have been obtained from a sacred quarry. This quarry seems to have been a sort of Mecca, to which every man from every part, was expected to journey once in his life, both for the sake of the pipe-bowl, and to satisfy the needs of his soul. It was, moreover, a universal Sanctuary, for according to an injunction from the Great Spirit at this quarry, there should be no blood shed : enemies would meet as friends.

All North American Indians were daring hunters and expert riders : some cultivated the soil but sparsely, trusting entirely to the products of Providence. It was this trust in the spirit of Nature which made them believe that it existed in various secret articles and forms, which, in the manner of a mascot, helped them in their under-takings ; it made them collect all kinds of odds and ends, to make what they called "good medicine." This included a specific antidote against someone else's "good medicine." One kind of "good medicine" ensured a good day's hunting, or a good day's killing, or success in any enterprise. This word, "good medicine," had a very wide meaning. All the Indian tribes hated and dreaded the white man, because his "good medicine" was superior to their own ; in other words, he had more knowledge, more enterprise, and was better equipped against misfortune.

Indian chiefs as well as others had collected all

kinds of articles which they called "good medicine," but if a medicine man, soothsayer, or
diviner professed to cure and failed, his medicine
became "bad medicine," and he was immediately
killed. A man's particular power of healing, or
his talisman, was revealed to him through a
dream, and apparently took the form of some
creature. As soon as he reached man's estate, he
retired to the woods, fasted, meditated, and
prayed to the Great Spirit that a vision of his
totem animal should be revealed to him. After
this vision appeared, he made every effort to
procure it ; and when he had done so, this mascot
was hung on his body for the remainder of his
life ; it was even buried with him, and accompanied
him to his happy hunting grounds. If it should
happen that he lost it, or was deprived of it by
an enemy, he could only acquire "good medicine"
and regain his former prestige by slaying another
man, and looting his "good medicine." Whatever
its imaginary properties may have been, it was
something that stimulated his bravery, and for
which he fought as he would for his own life.

The *Blackfeet* were the most numerous and
powerful of the tribes ; they were acknowledged
to number fifty thousand. Of middle stature, very
muscular, and deep chested, they spent a great
part of their time hunting for enemies among their
neighbours. In every tribe their wigwams were
so set up as to be removed at a moment's notice :
the mode of transport was by trailing large poles
tied to horses, on which were platforms ; dogs
were also used to trail smaller ones, a platform
being built proportional to their size.

The women of all tribes parted their hair in the
middle, and painted the line of separation with
vermilion. The men of the *Blackfeet* had two

partings on the top of the head, leaving a middle lock of hair about two inches wide : this " fringe " they allowed to hang as far as the bridge of the nose, when it was cut square. The skins they wore were dressed and usually dyed black, as also their footwear—hence the name " Blackfeet."

The *Crow* Indians were very near neighbours of the *Blackfeet,* but their language was totally different ; their hunting ground was at the head waters of the Missouri, and on the north-west of the Continent of the Indian groups ; they occupied their spare time in hunting for their neighbour's scalps, as well as losing a great number of their own ; consequently they became a rapidly diminishing people. All the skins with which they built and decorated their wigwams were ornamented with designs, illustrating their deeds of valour, while their tents were decorated with scalps and skulls.

The *Crows* were reputed to be a more honourable race than most of the other tribes. Their hair grew excessively long, sometimes dragging on the grass ; but not contented with that, they even promoted its growth by the constant use of bears' grease : " Long-hair," a chief of the tribe, had hair which measured 10 ft. 7 ins. long ; women cut their hair short. As a sign of mourning, it was customary for the men to cut off a lock or two, and for the women to cut theirs close to the scalp.

They appear to have been phlegmatic to the highest degree. Catlin relates how a chief, having been embellished and adorned with European clothes, by some person of distinction, returned to his tribe after a year's absence. For fully half an hour he stood before his wife and children, simply and purely that they might admire his elegant appearance ; during that time there was no symptom of recognition, or welcome, or satisfaction on either side ; but gradually each seemed to unbend, yet with no expression or emotion, until he at length seated himself among his wife and family, as though continuing a conversation of a year ago.

Except when boasting of any successful enterprise, they practised this art of reserve on all occasions, probably to conceal some weakness ; or, as some writers assert, to disguise an intense shyness or self-consciousness. This, however, only applied to tribal ethics, and included neither hunting, scalping, dancing, nor self-adornment, nor when they were acting in the rôle of an arbitrary chief.

The *Mandans* were a tribe in the Upper Missouri district, close to the boundary between America and Canada. They believed themselves to be the *first* people created on earth. Owing to the constant hunting for their neighbours' scalps, their numbers had diminished to a very considerable degree. They lived in lodges, in other words, in villages ; a number of lodges constituted a village, which was secured and fortified against any invasion of enemies. The floor of a lodge was two or three feet below the level of the ground, the materials being timber ; the lodge had walls and beams, and the roof and sides were covered with willow boughs ; the whole was plastered over with mud and clay. The slope of the roof was sufficiently flat on the outside, either to provide a resting place or a " look out." The lodges were made to hold about thirty people ; couches being arranged round the sides above the floor, while buffalo skins stretched over four posts formed the mattress. Along the side of each bed was a post studded with pegs, where the owner hung all his

MANDAN INDIANS.

precious belongings, and his " medicine " when he was asleep.

In the centre of the village was an open space, in which all sports and games and other functions were held ; and facing this space the " medicine " belonging to the tribe was kept in a barrel-shaped receptacle. Elsewhere, in the village, were long poles on which were scalps, with their long clinging hair waving like so many banners. Just behind the village was the burial place, called the village of the dead ; here, on a scaffolding, the bodies were placed, out of reach of wolves and dogs, and left to decay. The deceased was, however, prepared for burial, dressed in his best array ; and placed beside him, painted and oiled, was the dead man's pipe and tobacco, his bows and arrows, and a few days' provisions. His body was finally wrapped in fresh buffalo hide, and tightly bound from head to foot until he resembled a mummy ; he was then laid with his feet towards the East—the rising Sun.

For a long time after burial, the near relations of the departed man sat under this simple scaffolding, perhaps cutting and mutilating themselves to appease the spirits of the dead, for any acts of omission committed while he was on earth. When skeletons had fallen from the scaffolding, the skulls were preserved, and a ring of these would be formed in the prairie, with their faces looking towards the centre. In the middle of this ring was a small mound with a pole from which " medicine " hung, to protect and guard this sanctuary. Here, perhaps, long years afterwards, someone would pick up a piece of a skull, fondle it, and recount memories of a past when they were together in life. Here a mother would sit and work for hours, recounting to herself the story of its birth, the tales of its life, and recalling the anguish of its death.

Catlin is of the opinion that this group of people were the offspring of the aborigines of America, prior to the arrival of the North American Indians, for it is stated that there were many whose skins were almost white, one in ten of both sexes, and of every age, and who, from their infancy, had light silver grey hair, sometimes indeed almost white.

Mixed bathing was not permitted among the *Mandans*; when women and girls bathed, armed sentries were stationed to protect them from being abducted. After bathing, they thoroughly anointed themselves with bears' grease, massaging it well into their skin. The Indians felt it a great source of amusement, that Europeans were so stupid, as not to understand why they greased their bodies, slept with their feet towards the fire, or why they walked with their toes turned in.

Among all the Northern Indians, the chief of his tribe always wore an heraldic head-dress surmounted with buffalo horns; not only was it an emblem of rank, but also of authority, gained either by some deed of daring, influence, or power. These horns were so ingeniously secured to the headpiece as to give a certain dramatic effect, and to emphasize any point of oratory expressed by the additional action of the head. This custom seems to have originated through imitating the buffalo's toss of his head with its powerful horns, and to suggest by his magnificent strength —the emblem of Force.

Catlin relates that when he had painted the portrait of a man, he was accused of weakening that person. They declared that, owing to the extreme likeness, a chief was alive in two places.

This could only be possible if his existence in both places was halved. But if it was possible to remove half of a man, then the artist must have power to remove all he would, even the whole of a man ; therefore an artist was dangerous "medicine." Later, however, after a dog had been sacrificed to square the matter, everyone, especially the women, when dressed in their best, were anxious to see themselves reproduced on canvas.

Another universal custom of the North American Indians was for the host to wait on his guest ; the visitor's pipe was filled and lighted for him, and after the first draw, the host took a whiff from the same pipe ; then, and only then, did conversation commence. A chief enjoyed a plurality of wives, and on the occasion of a husband entertaining any company, the women sat round and looked on.

Polygamy was regarded both as an evidence of, and as a source of, wealth, for it was through the woman's labour of preparing skins for sale or barter, that a man acquired riches. Thus by acquiring wealth he was able to speculate in wives ; for, owing to the losses incurred in the sport of scalp hunting, there were nearly three times as many women as men, consequently, polygamy fitted very well into the situation. In nearly all cases women were bought from their fathers, their price being from one or two horses, a couple of gallons of whisky, and several pounds of beads. The *Mandan* girls married about the age of twelve or earlier ; whatever beauty they may have possessed very quickly vanished, owing to the heavy toil to which they were subjected ; amongst other duties, they fetched wood and water, cooked, dressed (chewed) all manners of skins, prepared meat, and dug the ground for the growing of corn.

The Indians had no stated time for their meals : there was always a pot stewing, and if any man, woman or child felt hungry they could help themselves. So long as this system was reciprocated, and each contributed to the contents of the pot, all went well ; but there were confirmed loafers and wasters, who never subscribed anything, and who helped no one.

These people aften ate in a reclining position. Women sat on their heels ; men sat cross-legged, and helped themselves first ; the remainder was given to the women, who consumed far more than the men. All meat was cut in long slices, and had been cured in the sun ; in this state it was called *pemican*.

The *Mandans'* dance suggested more a form of posing than dancing, almost corresponding to our Swedish drill, accompanied by yells and whoops, which gave it the aspect of suddenly becoming threatening. No doubt, at an early epoch, each step or posture suggested some meaning, probably connected with the chase, or stealth in head hunting ; but, possibly owing to the constant repetition, it became latterly, to the accompaniment of drums and a monotonous chant—merely a form of exercise and a display of agility.

The *buffalo dance* was a form of ritual to try and induce the herds of buffaloes to approach nearer, at the time when that kind of food was scarce. A number of the tribe, adorned with buffalo-horn headpieces, skipped up and down and yelled ; others began beating drums ; as each tired, another took his place, and this calling upon and soliciting the buffalo, continued until finally the beasts advanced near enough to be slaughtered.

Since the dance was for the definite purpose of coaxing the trusting animals it was bound to continue till they approached ; so it was always a success, although it might involve several weeks of dancing ; in fact, they danced for a purpose until they achieved it.

" Medicine " men went through a certain performance to produce rain. They burnt sweet-smelling herbs, projected an arrow into the air, or stood on the top of a wigwam gesticulating for hours ; they eventually succeeded, because they continued the farce, perhaps for several days, until it did rain.

Mandans had a great belief in self-sacrifice ; they would give up their most precious property to hang in the " medicine " tent.

Among these people there was an annual orgy of blood and fearful lacerations which served as a test of endurance among the budding youth ; as a picture of frightfulness was a test of fortitude at the sight of mangled men. Young men, emaciated with fasting, were, for the sake of fanaticism, skewered through the back or on the chest, and through their other limbs ; they were then swung round and round, while others added their weight by clinging to their bodies. Except as a final test of stoicism, their self-inflicted savagery had no meaning. This festival took place yearly, and many bore scars showing that they had gone through the ordeal on several occasions.

In spite of the severe tortures they bore on these religious ceremonies, the maimed would offer a sacrifice to the Great Spirit, with a devout prayer for more fortitude than they had already shown, for any future occasion of endurance ; they stoically submitted to the amputation of the little finger of the left hand ; sometimes they would also surrender to the Great Spirit the first finger.

Upon every occasion of feasts and festivals, the pipe was lighted ; before, however, it was smoked, the mouthpiece was turned upwards towards the Great Spirit, and was then pointed to the four cardinal points of the compass in succession— North, South, East and West—somewhat resembling the act of making the sign of the cross ; co-related to this, the number four was regarded as a mystic number.

It is deeply to be regretted that these interesting people were, in 1838, decimated by smallpox ; the handful left, but twenty, deliberately, for the purpose of suicide, braved thousands of *Sioux Indians* ; they all faced certain death, probably in the same stoical manner as when they tortured their flesh on the occasion of their annual festival. Thus they became extinct.

The *Sioux* (pronounced as a French word) were a numerous, tall, virile, and warlike tribe ; their name for themselves was *Dahkotas*. Inhabiting a vast tract of land, they were essentially nomadic, moving their hide-covered tents ; their migration over vast prairies, followed that of the animal and vegetable world. When, owing to food-shortage, their migrations became urgent, the old and feeble were left by the way. The able-bodied went through the ceremony of " Exposing "—in other words, they took a final leave of them. These derelicts and feeble ones would be placed under the shelter of a stretched buffalo skin, with a small fire and some firewood. Stoically, an aged man would say, " I am too old and too feeble to march ; I am an encumbrance and burden, and wish to die." These episodes, common to all Indian tribes, were what, under similar conditions, constitutes what would be termed an epic poem among civilized people ; such, for instance, as the act of Captain Oates, in Captain Scott's expedition to the South Pole, where he alluded to him as " a gallant gentleman."

A horse, deer skins, or buffalo robes were the usual objects of barter ; some ornaments composed of small bits of coloured shells called *Wampum*, which were used for war belts, became not only an article of barter, but a coinage, measured either in hand breadths, or fathoms (the length from the tips of the fingers of each hand, with the arm extended). After an imitation of this *Wampum*, made in Europe, was introduced to the Indians, its circulation as coinage ceased.

The value of a woman, as has been seen, was about two horses, with perhaps a few extras thrown in ; but after the death of one, Catlin relates how a father offered him ten horses for a painted picture of her. The same artist and author said, that the men could not understand why he should confer such an honour on a woman as to make a picture of her, and that under no circumstances should the portraits of men be exhibited with those of women. This attitude seems curious, when it may be noted that the death-rate among the tribes was very great, while the birth-rate was diminishing, which depended on the very existence and numerical strength of the tribe.

The *Alguoguins* made a distinction between the wife whom they called " The entrance of the hut," and those whom they termed " The middle of the hut " ; these last were servants and of inferior rank.

Dogs were the Indians' best companions ; they hunted together, they shared the produce of the chase; the dog was his watcher and sentinel, and the image of the dog, as they painted him on their deer-skins and robes, was the emblem of fidelity. In paying the highest honour to a visitor, he would sacrifice what he cherished most; and the food on this occasion would be his dog; in fact, the dog feast would be the scene of the most solemn ceremony, in sealing a pledge, or in appeasing evil spirits.

Their smoking mixture was called *K'nick K'nick*.

Orpheus and his lute had passed the fable stage, among these Indians : they made a flute, much resembling our tin flute, on which three or four musical notes, without any particular interval, could be produced. The instrument was called the *Winnebago* courting flute; a youth sat on a rock or a log, and repeated the order of certain notes persistently, calling the attention of his sweetheart to his presence, until it pleased her to come to him.

Dancing, if that was the name of the form of violent exercise by which they amused themselves, was frequently enjoyed; the accompaniment was the usual primitive drum, and voices, for encouragement. The steps consisted of jumps, as well as contortions of the body and face, with yelps and screams. These primitive dances partook of the idea which they desired to represent, much of the meaning of these caperings being symbolical. Only men were performers; women derived the enjoyment of being worked up to an enthusiasm for laughter by looking on. There would be a " *Bear dance*," in which the spirit of the bears was appealed to; also the " *Scalp dance*," the name of which speaks for itself.

The Northern Indians differed in appearance from any other tribe, having small noses, low fore-

heads, high cheek bones, full cheeks, Roman
noses, and, usually, broad chins.   The men seldom
grew any beard until they reached middle age ;
even then it was a scanty appearance, but remarkably strong and bristly.   As it was considered
unsightly, and not conducive to their good looks,
many pulled it out between the finger and the
blunt edge of a knife.

The Indians in *Hudson's Bay* suffered such acute
pangs of hunger that they were frequently reduced
to cannibalism.   Mr. Hearne thus described several
of these unfortunate wretches : " A smile never
graced their countenances . . . while the eye
most expressively spoke the dictates of the heart,
and seemed to say ' Why do you despise me for
my misfortunes ?   The period is probably not far
distant when you may be driven to the like
necessity.' "

The *Copper Indians* were evidently in complete
ignorance as to the appearance of an Englishman
until they beheld Mr. Hearne.   On the whole they
agreed that he was a perfect human being, with
the exception of his hair and eyes ; the former,
they said, reminded them of the stained hair of a
buffalo's tail ; the latter being light resembled
those of a gull.   They also spoke slightingly of
the colour of his skin, declaring that it was like
meat which had been rendered sodden by being
put into water, until all the blood had been
extracted.   Taking him all round, he was regarded
as such a curiosity, that whenever he combed his
hair he was begged for the combings, which were
carefully wrapped up; at the same time they said,
" When I see you again, you shall again see your
hair."

The morals of the North Americans were somewhat shady ; it was quite an ordinary occurrence

for the men to exchange a night's lodging with one
of their friend's wives. And, far from it being
regarded as an insult, it cemented friendships
between families ; and if one man died, the other
was most scrupulous in looking after the children
of the deceased.

A strong antipathy existed from all time between
the *Copper Indians* and the Esquimaux. We read
of how, on one occasion, the Esquimaux were
brutally massacred by the Indians, when peace-
fully sleeping, who, before they committed this
cowardly onslaught painted their shields or targets
to the very edge, with different images ; the sun,
moon, birds and beasts of prey ; hieroglyphics and
imaginary figures, believed to be the inhabitants
of the earth, sea, air, etc. Each one painted what
he considered would be most likely to secure him
success in his undertaking.

After the murder of the Esquimaux, the Indians
who had touched the slain, went through a strange
method of purification : they were forbidden from
cooking any food either for themselves or others.
Those who were under the ban when food had
been prepared, painted their faces between the
nose and chin, and most of their cheeks with a
sort of red earth, before they would taste a morsel ;
they also refused to eat of any dish but their own,
or smoke out of anyone else's pipe.

Mr. Hearne avows, in spite of having no con-
firmation, that on still nights he actually heard
the Northern Lights make a rustling and crackling
noise, like a large flag flapping in the wind. The
Northern Indians never buried their dead, so by
many it was believed that they fell a prey to
birds or animals ; for this reason they never ate
foxes, ravens, etc., unless from necessity. After
the death of a near relative, they wept repeatedly

for a year, the time being measured by moons and seasons ; even during eating and conversation they made a sort of howling noise ; they also cut their hair and rent their clothing. Of religion, they had practically none, nor any idea of a future existence ; they had their superstitions and their diviners ; probably, also, their totem animals, for they would sometimes upbraid their children for speaking disrespectfully of some beast or bird.

In the late autumn men usually painted the mouth and part of the cheek before each meal ; during this time they must never embrace their wives or children, nor eat certain parts of the deer. But when winter set in, a man unseen by any woman, lit a fire some way from the tents, into which were thrown all their ornaments, pipe-stems and dishes. After which a grand banquet was prepared, at which they ate all that had previously been forbidden. They might also embrace their wives and children " at discretion," which limitation had, from what we understand, a wide margin.

Among these Northern Indians, as well as the *Copper* and *Dog-ribbed Indians*, they had three or four parallel black strokes on each cheek, made by running a needle or awl under the skin, and upon drawing it out immediately rubbing in powdered charcoal. Their dispositions were far from attractive, for they were morose, covetous, and hypocritical, yet the mildest tribe of Indians.

As a rule, the men were extremely jealous of their wives, who were usually mere children ; these unfortunate children, from the age of eight or nine, were forbidden the most harmless amusements with the opposite sex ; instead of which custom dictated that they should be watched and guarded, cooped up with old women, and occupied in scraping skins, mending shoes, and suchlike

household duties.   Divorces were fairly common ;
the girls had first a good pummelling, then were
turned adrift, and told to rejoin their paramours
or relatives as the case might be.   It is as well,
perhaps, that these people, as in Greenland, were
not prolific.

No form of cradle was used for infants ; as with
the Southern Indians, a lump of moss was tied
between the legs of their offspring, who were thus
carried on their mothers' backs, next to their
skin.   When girls became of a marriageable age,
they wore for some little time a kind of veil, or
curtain made of beads, as a sign of modesty.

Should two parties of these Indians meet, they
came to a sudden halt about twenty or thirty
yards apart, and either sat or lay down for several
minutes.   Then an elderly man, should there be
one amongst them, held forth as to all his misfortunes since last they met ; also recounting all
the deaths and misfortunes of any other Indians
of which he might have heard.   Then the most
elderly man on the other side began his tale of
woe and tribulation.   If these became too harrow-
ing universal howls were then commenced, an art
in which young girls were specially expert.   After
a short time, however, tobacco was handed round,
and conversation drifted on to good news ; so that
in less than half an hour smiles were on every face,
and small gifts frequently exchanged.

The amusements of these people were few ; they
had an out-door game played with short clubs,
sharpened at one end, called *holl*, which slightly
resembles quoits.   Sometimes, at night, they
amused themselves with dancing, although they
had no dances or songs of their own ; but they
tried to imitate the *Dog-ribbed* dances ; these were
easy to learn, as they consisted only of lifting the

CAPTAIN COOK'S TRAVELS.

feet from the ground as quickly, and as high as possible, without moving the body ; the hands kept closed, and close to the breast, the head inclining forward. This dance was always performed in a state of nudity except for the " breech-cloth " which was also sometimes flung off.

The vocal music accompaniment consisted only of a repetition, such as " hee hee, ho ho," etc., which, by raising and lowering the voice, and dwelling sometimes longer, sometimes shorter, on a word, produced the resemblance of a tune.   The dancing was accompanied by a drum or *tabor* ; or sometimes by a rattle, made from dried buffalo skin, into which shot or pebbles had been placed and shaken about.   The dancing of the women was still more monotonous, for they crowded outside the tent in a straight line, and shuffled from right to left, and back in the same line.   When the music stopped, they bent slightly as though making an awkward sort of curtsey, pronouncing in a shrill voice, " hee, hoooe."

When any of the important Northern Indians died, it was believed that it was through the evil machinations of either some of their own people, the Southerners, or particularly the Esquimaux. They did not bury their dead, which were devoured by the wild beasts and birds.   Should the deceased be a near relation, they rent their clothing, and mourned for a year.

They held a curious tradition that the first person who lived on earth was a woman, who in her searches after berries, which was her only food, met with an animal resembling a dog, which grew attached to her and followed her to the cave where she lived.   This dog possessed the peculiar faculty of transforming itself into a handsome young man at night, although always resuming

its old shape in the daytime ; so the woman looked
upon the strange happenings as so many dreams
and delusions. But matters arrived at a point
which could not be ignored, as the mother of the
world advanced in her condition of productive-
ness.

Not long after this, a man appeared, of such
surprising height that his head touched the
clouds, for the purpose of levelling the land, which
he did by the help of his walking-stick. He
marked out the rivers, lakes, and ponds, and
caused them to be filled up with water. Next, he
took the dog and tore it to pieces ; its entrails
he threw into the lakes and rivers, commanding
them to become fish. The flesh he threw over the
land, ordering it to become various kinds of beasts ;
while the skin he tore into small pieces, throwing
them into the air, and decreed that they might
become all manner of birds. He finally gave the
woman and her offspring power to kill, eat, and
never spare, for he had commanded that she should
be supplied abundantly with all she desired.
After this, he returned to the place from whence
he came, and has never been heard of since.

Old age was the greatest catastrophe which
could befall the Northern Indians, for even by
their own children they were treated with dis-
respect, served last at meals, given the worst and
poorest of the food ; while the coarsest of their
skins served for their old parents ; they might
even die of starvation and neglect. These people
believed in different kinds of fairies called *Nant-e-
na*, whom they imagined inhabited the various
elements of earth, sea, and air, and whom they
frequently declared they saw.

The *Aurora Borealis* they called *Ed-thin*, that is
Deer. For experience had shown them that when

a hairy deerskin was briskly stroked with the hand on a dark night, it gave out sparks of electrical fire.   And when the meteor was very bright in the planet, they said there were many deer in that part of the atmosphere, although, as Hearne shrewdly observes—they had not yet extended their beliefs to such a point as to indulge in any hopes of tasting this celestial animal.

THE NORTHERN REGIONS AND GREENLAND

THE famous explorer, Captain Ross, in his expedition of discovering a North West passage into the Pacific Ocean in 1818, came across a few native Esquimaux ; and through the aid of a Greenlander on board, was able to converse with them, and learn something of their beliefs and customs. They are described as being of a dirty copper colour, about five feet in height, fat, and squarely built ; their dress consisted of seal, deer, and bear skins. Although only eighteen of these people were seen, they pointed to the north, and said there were "plenty of people" there. The amazement of these Esquimaux, when they first beheld the Europeans and a ship, can well be imagined, for they had always believed that they were the only human beings in the world, the rest being ice. It was also a matter of astonishment to them, that there were no women on board the ships of Captain Ross. There was much for them yet to learn, even their power of counting did not extend beyond ten.

In their primitive state, we hear dark stories of cannibalism, infanticide, and other crimes ; it was unsafe for ships to land on their shores. Cranty tells us that in 1740 a Dutch brig was captured, and the whole crew massacred. These people seem to have had an inner conception of a Supreme Being, but it was vague and undefinable.

Their houses were six feet in height, built half underground of stone, and "mudded" to prevent the damp from getting in ; on the floor, skins were thrown. Several families lived in one house, each keeping a lamp burning, never allowed to go out, and which served for purposes of cooking as well as for heating. Their staple food was the liver and blubber of the walrus and seal ; but as winter darkness approached, and the ice froze, as a last resource to prevent starvation, they ate their daily companions, their dogs ; surely not a very remote step from their uncles and aunts, and even nearer relatives.

The regulated ceremonies of mourning for the dead, were curious ; to use Dr. Kane's words : " they weep according to system " ; one person commenced and all were expected to join. It was the official right of the most distinguished among the company, to wipe the eyes of the chief mourner. There were frequent weeping gatherings ; at other times, someone would be suddenly convulsed by sobs, the others following politely, although perhaps quite ignorant of the particular source of grief.

It was not indeed necessary that death only should produce such abandonment of sorrow ; the failure of a hunt, the snapping of a walrus line, etc., would have the same result. But occasionally there entered a totally different reason for mourning : for the ancient Esquimaux believed that death was sometimes caused by supernatural agencies, and that some form of conciliation was necessary to pacify these offended powers. The *Angekok*, or medicine man, who claimed supernatural attributes, regulated the period and penances of grief ; the stricken husband might be forbidden to take part in the walrus hunt for a whole year, or to abstain from one of their meagre luxuries.

Among their many avocations, the *Angekok* professed to communicate with spirits. It was they, who, after protracted fasts and meditations, became the medium of communication with the spirits. By working themselves into an hysterically inspired condition, they claimed to hold communion with those not of this earth; to prophesy according to their visions.

As well as the *Angekok*, there were the *Issiutoks*, but these worked evil spells and incantations; they were treated in the same brutal manner as the witches of old. Having been harpooned and mutilated, small portions of their heart were eaten, to make sure that this man of the " evil eye " could not return to earth unrecognized.

One of the curious customs of the Esquimaux who lived in Hudson's Bay, was that the men had all the hair of their dead plucked out by the roots, to distinguish them from every other tribe.

Their native dance consisted more in motions of the hands than of the feet; the latter were kept close together, occasional jumps being given, while with the arms, a continual swinging motion was maintained. Their small eyes being usually closed during the dance gave them a most sheepish look.

Their teeth were very bad and worn down to the gums, especially in the women; this was due to their chewing the skins, which constituted their dresses, to make them pliable for wear.

At *Peteravik* the dead were sewn up in skins with their limbs outstretched. Should the deceased be a woman, her husband carried her, unattended, to her last resting-place, where he piled up stones over her one by one, to form a cairn. In the meantime the blubber lamp was kept burning; then the mourners assembled beside the cairn to lament and howl, while the widower recounted the virtues of his wife, and his own devastating sorrow.

Esquimaux were usually buried with their knees

drawn close to their bodies; desolation is the word which best describes that last scene. As Dr. Kane observes—there was no Mother Earth to receive the dead; so their companions encased their bodies in sacks of skins, and grouped their implements around them; over all were placed a pile of stones and a cairn. We are told that the Esquimaux never disturbed a grave.

Greenland was discovered by a Norwegian called *Torwald* in 982, when driven out of Iceland. The sight of the green vegetation, during the season of spring appearing along the coast, suggested to the discoverer the name of Green land. It was revisited about seven or eight centuries ago. Some authorities suggest that these people originated from Tartary. In 1742, a trading station was established by the Danes in Frédéric Shaab. The first known community of these natives assembled at a place called God's Shaab in 1721. In 1730, the native population was estimated to be about 30,000, divided into a dozen communities.

There is an eight months' winter in that land, the autumn winds being so violent that houses are blown down, while tents, and even small boats, are lifted up and carried a long distance. Indeed, Greenlanders assert that these cyclones have raised stones of 2 lbs. weight from the ground, and when it was necessary for a man to go out, he was obliged to crawl on his hands and knees.

Similar cyclones occur in summer, the season of no night. At this period of the year the natives hunt and fish throughout the hours which we call night. On the other hand, from a certain latitude towards the north, there is for months no daylight visible; but the light of both the moon and stars is much more brilliant than in more temperate zones, where the atmosphere is less rarefied

In these ice-covered lands, the Aurora Borealis, wondrous mirages, and subjects of dreamland are all represented upside down.

Asbestos is found in this country ; the natives use this mineral for lamp-wicks ; also as a funeral envelope, within which they bury their dead. A particular kind of moss grows which the people use for a bread. According to Cranty it is anything but palatable, but leaves a pleasant flavour in the mouth. As Nature had provided the Greenlanders with no other means of subsistence, they were forced to be both hunters and fishermen ; and for mutual aid, in both, as well as for protection against wild beasts, more especially the Polar bear, they live in communities.

This land of storms and electric pictures could not fail in having diviners, ranging from medicine men to soothsayers ; these sorcerers impressed on the fishermen that to successfully combat a whale, it was necessary to wear their best and cleanest apparel ; for, said they, if anyone wore soiled clothing, or had touched any dead object the whale would most assuredly escape or, when wounded, sink to the bottom of the sea. Thus, from canoes, men and women attacked the whale with harpoons, to which were attached inflated seal-skins, used as buoys, in such a manner as to prevent the whale from diving.

In appearance, Greenlanders much resemble the Esquimaux ; in addition we are told their faces are round and flat, with high cheek bones and very beady eyes ; their mouths are small, with a large under lip.

They are, moreover, copper coloured, with a rich coating of dirt, mixed with oil and fat. What else could be expected, considering they lived in a chronic atmosphere of grease and oil, and seldom

or never washed ; although we hear that after a
long fishing expedition the men dipped their
fingers in fresh water, and wiped the salt out of
their eyes. Their eating habits, too, were excessively dirty ; their cooking utensils were licked
clean by the dogs, while their knives scraped off
remnants of food from their mouths, teeth, and
fingers.

Unlike most hunters, who then and there
devoured the beast they had slain, these people
merely drank some of the warm blood, and ate
only a small piece of the flesh. After the day's
toil was ended, the unsuccessful hunters or fishermen partook equally with the more fortunate.
All food was consumed that same day, no allowance
being made for a possible disastrous to-morrow,
nor for bad seasons. Under such a happy-go-
lucky existence, it was not surprising that, sometimes for days at a time, they were entirely
without food. The climax was reached when they
subsisted only on the soles of their boots, or even
on their tent skins, boiled in the oil which was
usually burnt in their lamps.

The women were specially sturdy ; this enabled
them to carry the weighty burdens, so essential
to the existence of the tribe.

In regard to the dress of these people, when
outside their tent, the neck and throat were left
exposed to the weather ; but inside they stripped
to the waist ; yet, whether clothed or semi-nude,
the Danish missionaries had to make the most
superhuman efforts to submit to the stench of a
congregation of Greenlander humanity.

There seems to have been an absence of all
individuality among these people ; all were
phlegmatic and tranquil, almost to the stage of
melancholy or stupidity. Life was sufficient unto

the day, yesterday was already forgotten, to-morrow had not yet arrived. In this state of self-complacency, they had a certain contempt for Europeans ; although they admitted that they were more industrious, intelligent, possessed a greater variety of property than themselves. Yet, they failed in seeing wherein lay the pleasure of any of these things. In our times a similar comparison could be made between the life of a gipsy with that of a stock-broker with a fine mansion in a fashionable neighbourhood. The Greenlanders' occupation was whaling, seal fishing, or bear and deer hunting, etc. ; and, given a sufficiency of this for their subsistence, of what use was anything more ? Why the loss of temper and uncalled for energy they observed among their visitors ?

Excessive patience was a necessity to their success in hunting, and immobility of body in one particular position was the only camouflage possible in approaching their prey. On account of the rigour of the climate, and the sterility of the soil, they could never remain long idle ; during the protracted days they only hunted five or six hours ; in the never-ending nights for an hour at the utmost. But whether they worked or watched during the night, they slept most of the day.

These people lived in tents during the summer, but in houses of stone plastered with earth in winter ; these were not built below ground, but, for choice, on the summit of a hillock, or on a single rock, in order not to be entirely snowed up. So long as the temperature was below freezing, these houses were adequate enough, but summer rains occasionally washed away the cementing material, in which case they had to be rebuilt before the following autumn.

These houses were so devised, that the inmates had to enter them on their hands and knees ; the walls were lined with hides, which had been previously used for canoes or tents. Each of these buildings held from three to six families, who slept in a sitting position, leaning against a bench on which cooking utensils were placed ; the men with their feet resting on the floor, the women sitting cross-legged. Windows made from the intestines of fish, were let into the walls, which were sufficiently transparent to let in a moderate amount of light. A lamp fed with whale oil, served the same purposes as for the Esquimaux.

It is said that, what with oil lamps, fish and meat stewing, combined with other insanitary arrangements, these houses would certainly have overpowered a European ; yet here, a community of natives lived not only in good health, but in absolute self-satisfied contentment.

Nature was more generous to these people in their covering than in their food : for vests they used either deer skins, or the skins of water birds (penguins), the down being worn inside ; stockings were manufactured from the skins of unborn seals. Over all, was a garment in the shape of a sailor's jumper, usually low-necked with long sleeves and a hood, reaching to the knees. Fishermen's clothing was made in one piece, and so water-tight that De la Harpe tells us it acted as a life-buoy, in case their canoe should be swamped.

Owing, no doubt, to the coldness of the climate, the relation between the sexes was apathetic rather than ardent. Conversation flagged between them—in reality there was little to say. Their laws of etiquette were somewhat rigid ; were a young man to offer a maiden a pinch of tobacco, it would be regarded as a great insult. Youths

seldom married before they were about twenty, and
girls were about the same age.   The marriage rites
of the Greenlanders was the ancient one of marriage
by capture.   Consent having been obtained from
the parents, the bride was fetched from her
home by several women, under pretence of force.
On arriving at her husband's house, she betook
herself into a corner, and with dishevelled hair,
she covered her face with well studied abasement.
In course of time, however, she became less
unapproachable, and the marriage was concluded.

   There was no *dot* to be settled in these nuptials ;
indeed, the bridegroom's only possessions were his
skins, his knife, and his lamp.   His qualifications
were his skill as a good hunter or fisherman ; the
bride on her part did the hundred and one things
expected of a woman in these parts, except that
occasionally she had no progeny ; in which case
the husband was allowed to take another wife.
There was little difficulty in obtaining a divorce ;
the man had merely to give his spouse a peevish
look, pack up her clothes, and return her to her
friends, where she would conduct herself with such
exceeding modesty as would bring her husband
into great ill-repute.   Cutting off the hair was a
serious barrier to matrimony, the lack of hair
being regarded as a great disgrace.

   Wives seldom bore more than three or four
children, and any symptom of fecundity was
regarded with disapproval, as showing a certain
measure of wantonness.   Names were more or less
hereditary, but nicknames were acquired through
any peculiarity.   Should a man of a similar name
die, it was customary for a man to assume another
name, in any case until the memory of the deceased
had considerably waned. Parents were never
known to strike a child, and children were stated

to be devoid of any form of viciousness ; moreover, in the communal manner in which these people lived, lying to one another would be devoid of any object. Children were, therefore, both by heredity and by force of circumstance, strictly honest and truthful amongst each other. As soon as a boy was able to handle such things, he used a bow and arrows, and was never without a toy knife. When he was about ten years old, he was given a canoe (*Kajak*) in which he learnt to fish ; at his first success in seal and walrus fishing he was acclaimed by all the women, and declared a man.

A man's part in the affairs of life was doing all the needful hunting and fishing, but it was beneath his dignity either to carry or to skin his captures —this was woman's work. A great number of things were women's work : amongst others making clothes, building huts, and cooking food. Indeed, from the day she was married until the day of her death, the life of a woman was made up of incessant labour—sometimes, indeed, of days and weeks of starvation and misery. Owing to their strenuous life of exposure in all weathers, men seldom lived beyond fifty ; women lived longer, and so, with such a superfluity of women, polygamy obviously followed.

These people had a definite season for purposes of barter ; the Southerners had no whales, the Northerners no wood, and the mart was perhaps 400 miles midway. When these expeditions were undertaken, each party made the journey accompanied by their whole family, taking with them all their worldly possessions. And here entered a very important factor regarding all emigrations ; for if, wind and weather-bound, any group were isolated or marooned, they might amalgamate or form another separate tribe in new lands. Among themselves it was well known, that after or during these yearly ventures, some might return after long periods of voyaging, others had gone for ever. It is curious to hear that the most valued article of barter between the natives and Europeans was snuff—a man would sell all the clothing on his back for a small quantity of snuff.

One of their games, the main object being apparently to enable them to endure pain, was to hammer at one another, in turns, on the back, with clenched fists. He who endured this hammering the longest was the conqueror ; even then his endurance was put to a further test with a new competitor—until he succumbed ; thus, in course of time, each one was knocked out.

In their most stormy quarrels the dispute was settled by a systematic wrangling debate, each having a number of supporters listening to, and enjoying the mutual recriminations, and unconstrained ridicule of satire and raillery. Yet in spite of this exhibition of mutual disdainful scorn, no violent adjectives were used ; and the duel of words being ended, all was harmony once more.

The people of the Arctic Regions were obviously Sun Worshippers, for that orb meant everything to them ; at the winter solstice they contorted their bodies and danced frantically, keeping up the revel for several days until they were completely exhausted.

There were certain laws accepted by all, in connection with the hunt, fishing, or what was cast up on the shore ; for example, anyone finding wood of any kind, or parts of a wreck, was, on bringing it to the land, considered the legal owner of that prize, and no one would think of removing the stone he placed on it. In the case of fishing, so long as the harpoon with the rope attached still stuck into the fish, it was the property of the owner of the harpoon, although the fish may have got away with the weapon; but if the rope became detached from the harpoon, the fish became the property of the one who caught it, but he returned the harpoon to its owner. Should a whale be washed up on the shore, it became common property, one and all slashing pieces out of it.

The communal customs relating to all possible cases seemed so fair and just, that Mr. Cranty, the Moravian missionary, in 1733, was reluctant in disturbing these inoffensive people by the introduction of the orthodox laws of Christianity which he brought with him from Europe. They had, he said, learnt too well the most callous acts of Nature; like the animals none would assist another, drowning, or starving, or in distress; Nature was manifestly unsympathetic, inadequate, often unnecessarily cruel; the battle of life always favoured the strong; men ruled over women; women over children; children over birds.

The cult of Metamorphosis was a source of great consolation to these people. If a father chanced to lose his son, a widow persuaded him that the soul of his son had passed into one of her children lately born; in this case the man adopted both the widow and her offspring as his own.

A Greenlander's Paradise was at the bottom of the sea, where, from the bowels of the earth, it supported all the water above them. Here was an eternal summer with perpetual daylight; the waters were always clean, and there abounded unlimited game and fish, which, without the effort of man, fell into his pots always ready filled with boiling water; but it was only those who had performed their service in this world, who entered this Elysium. To reach this Paradise the soul glided for five days over rugged rocks which were covered in blood ; it may be that this last function of the soul had been derived from some idea of a Purgatory, that was grafted into their minds many centuries before by some European travellers. In addition to this tenet, they also believed that the soul itself in its perilous journey through Purgatory, ran the risk of annihilation ; it was especially for this reason, that the deceased's parents abstained for five days from certain foods, and did not raise their voices beyond a whisper during their daily work, so as not to distress nor tire the soul in its journey.

Others located Paradise in the sky above the clouds ; the soul being able to fly to the stars, its first resting-place was the Moon, where it mingled with other spirits. The wondrous Northern Lights represented to the Greenlanders the dance of souls. This conception seems to have been a survival of a very ancient belief, credited more among the Southerners than the Northerners.

They believed in two Spirit Principles : one good, the other evil. It was the Good Principle the diviners consulted in regard to the future. Some believed he was indefinite, without form ; others, more materialistic, that he was like a gigantic bear ; or that he resembled a man but had only one arm, or that he had more the form of a dove. The Bad Principle was feminine ; this goddess resided in a submerged palace, and by her magic enslaved all the fish and dwellers of the sea. She was guarded by a Cerberus, who never slept. In the case of shortage of sea food, the diviner had to propitiate this malevolent goddess.

The female Principle was not favoured by the Greenlanders ; it was a melancholy spirit which attached itself to man. Apart from these Great

Principles were a host of minor ones, connected with the success or failure of their undertakings, either encouraging or opposing them. There were also mountain genii, and fairy dwarfs ; and a spirit of fresh water streams—the first drink from such pure rivulets would drive out any evil spirit of which the drinker might be possessed.

It is a peculiar characteristic, a phase in the evolution of all mankind, in all parts of the world, to be so credulous as to believe in the power of charms and amulets. These mascots worn by men, women and children were believed to possess a kind of guardian spirit which preserved the wearer from danger or sickness, and generally brought about good luck : curious pieces of wood, or stones ; a bone, a bird's feather hanging round the neck ; or bits of hide dangling from the arms, or on the chest, were some of these mascots.

Moreover, the value of the mascot would be enhanced were it a gift ; if given by a European, whether a small strip of his clothing, or even a piece of his boot, through that gift would permeate the spirit of his country. A native will often beg a European to breathe over him. All kinds of charms were hung from their huts and their canoes, and no fisherman would start out without the special mascot to bring him good luck, and to save him from drowning.

At this date (1730) there was no written language, because the people could not understand ; they were even frightened to carry a written message. Altogether, on many points, the Greenlanders were sorely handicapped. Since there was no sun visible in winter, there was no possible means of recording the time of day ; but by observing the first faint rays of light on the summit of the inland mountains, they had an approximate idea of the time of mid-winter ; when this was recorded they

held their New Year's festival. During the three
following moons they prepared to shift out of
their winter quarters ; at their fourth moon some
small bird visitors began to arrive ; when the
walrus or sea horse appeared it was the fifth moon.
At this period they partly lost sight of the moon
through the following twenty-four hours, owing to
the brilliance of the sun. When the moon was
not visible they counted the days by the length
of the shadows cast by the rocks ; although by
the shortest daily shadow they were only able to
tell when it was midday or the longest day.

The stars, they said, were the spirits of deceased
Greenlanders ; shooting stars were souls on their
way to visit hell, to discover what was taking
place there. Their knowledge of astronomy was
used partly as a guide to the seasons, embellished
with fable and poetry ; for example, the three stars
forming what we call Orion's Belt, were represented
to the Greenlander as three men, who, having lost
their way after sea-horse fishing, were transported
into the sky. The Sun and Moon were represented as brother and sister ; the marks in the
Moon were made by her brother's soiled and
greasy fingers, and by these smears he would be
able to recognize her. Thunder was produced by
two women quarrelling over a seal's skin ; during
the squabble the house collapsed, the lamps were
broken, and produced lightning.

The use of snuff alleviated many of the eye
troubles so prevalent in the land. When a man
was buried his canoe, bow and arrows were placed
by his side ; when a woman was buried her
needles and knife were placed near her body ;
and on the grave of a child was placed the head
of a dog, for without its assistance the child would
have been incapable of finding its way.

PERSIA

ABOUT 1650 Persia extended from the Caspian Sea to the Indian Ocean, was bordered on the east by the Mongols of China, and on the west by the Euphrates, Ispaham being the capital. Tavernier describes the streets as inconceivably dirty, littered with every form of garbage, and open sewerage ; beasts were slaughtered in the main thoroughfare, others left to die there. Little wonder was it, therefore, that the better classes always travelled on horseback.

Cleanliness did not in other respects appeal to the Persians. Morier tells us of a Persian repast, of which the company partook seated on their customary mat or carpet, their feet tucked under them. They placed their chins close to the dishes, and scooped up the food with their three fingers and the thumb of the right hand. On the ground was placed the *sofra* or the tablecloth, which had been so long in use that its fragrance was remarkably unsavoury ; the Persians were wholly indifferent to this fact, declaring that " changing the *sofra* brings ill-luck."

Among their amusements they played a game with eggs ; this consisted in butting the ends against each other ; strong eggs were, therefore, a valuable asset ; marionette shows were also very popular. Their dances, writes Edward Stoll Waring, were crudely indecent and disgusting, but their songs were beautiful and pathetic, the usual theme being praise of wine and beauty, and the cruelty of their mistresses. Many of the nobler orders engaged Georgian boys to sing, and play on different instruments.

The Persian considered it part of his religion to

be vigilant in guarding both his faith and his
wives. It was criminal even to look at the
habitations of neighbours' wives; their jealousy
reached such a point that they built a hut over
the graves of their women, so that no man might
even catch a glimpse of the lifeless remains. They
also instilled into the minds of their wives, that
not only should they shun the society of the other
sex, but that they should avoid even looking at
them. They believed that when the faithful are
in Paradise, they will have eyes in the crown of
their head, to prevent them seeing the *houris*, or
celestial women who belong to others.

Neither were married women, unless of a very
low class, allowed to see their nephews or their
husband's brothers; indeed brothers were frequently forbidden to see their sisters. When the
women paid visits, a troupe of horsemen rode
before them crying *Kuruck! Kuruck!* in order
that no man might be in the path; otherwise he
would be beaten with the staves of these out-
runners. Should a man be found in the path of
the King's harem, he would immediately be put
to death. Upon the route of these ladies becoming
known, all the men near the path taken by the
harem were obliged to leave their houses.

Espoused wives were called *Nekaa*, four being
allowed by the Mahometan law; but, owing to
the expense, men very seldom had more than one.
"If they cannot content themselves," says
Chardin, "with one women, which *is* a misfortune
that never fails to befall 'em, they make use of
their slaves. By that means the Peace of the
Family is never disquieted: for the marry'd
wife . . . whether contented or no, her Relations
never take any notice."

If, by chance, a person of quality fell in love

with a woman unfitted to be his wife from a social
point of view, he hired her for ninety-nine years,
so that he made sure of her during his life.
Persians were usually married through a half-
opened door which separated the bride from her
bridegroom ; a priest, or someone possessing the
necessary authority, stretched out his hand to the
bride elect, saying, " I, authorized proxy for you,
marry you to him. You shall be his perpetual
wife with such dowry according as you have
agreed " ; the same formula was then quoted
from the husband's side.

"About an hour after she had been at her
husband's house, the matrons carry her into the
bridal chamber, uncloath her to a little waste-coat,
and put her to bed." When the bridegroom
entered all the lights were extinguished ; we also
hear that " Coyness frequently happens among
persons of quality . . . those of the blood royal,
more particularly, put their husbands to this
trouble, so that it requires whole months to
reclaim 'em." Sometimes the haggling over the
dowry took place up to the time of the delivery of
the maid to the man ; in such cases, it being a
dishonour to return home, the bride's parents were
obliged to accept a reduction. Chardin com-
ments : " We may say in general that the matches
are more happy in a country where the man and
woman never see one another ; then the women
are coveted."

Persians frequently changed their names, either
to give them greater dignity, or in hopes of better
fortune. In 1667, the first year of the monarch's
rule had so many misfortunes on account of war
and famine, that he was induced to change his
name. The prince was therefore crowned afresh
under the name of Soliman ; and all the old seals

and coins bearing the name of Sefi were destroyed as though he had died.

Sir John Chardin says : " The women more frequently change their names than the men, whether owing to a natural inconsistency, or that they do not agree to the alterations they find in life, being put upon them on account of their beauty, gaiety, their agility in dancing, or fine voice . . . they assume other names which better agree to their changed state."

Kings never allowed malefactors to look at them ; for this reason their faces were always covered when in his majesty's presence.

The Persians had very beautiful horses which were brought from Armenia ; the " crown royal " was set on the head of a horse, as victorious (triumphant) chariots were also crowned.

The Persian ladies, says Olearius, did not wear their two or three rows of pearls round their necks but on their heads, beginning at the forehead and going down the cheeks, and beneath the chin, giving an appearance as though their faces were set in pearls. From the belief that married people had a particularly happy life in a future state, they used often to hire persons to be espoused to those who had died unwed.

When a man desired to find a wife for his son, he went to the house of the damsel he had selected ; should her father have sweetmeats produced, it was taken for a sign that the overtures had been favourably received. The usual presents were then offered by the bridegroom, which, if he was in fairly good circumstances, usually consisted of two suits of fine clothes, a sum of money for the benefit of his bride, in case of a divorce, and a looking-glass ; the contract was afterwards signed by the Cadi or Magistrate.

On the night of the wedding the bride was
attired in a dress of red silk, or painted muslin ;
the bridegroom then sent for a horse for her to
mount ; and one of the bridesmaids held up a
looking-glass in front of her, all the way to her
husband's house, in order that she might see
herself for the last time as a maid. A large
procession followed, and the marriage festivities
lasted eight or ten days. Chardin (1684) declares
that matrimony in Persia was very expensive, so
that "Persons of Estates will not venture upon
it." Mahometans took their wives after three
methods : (1) by purchase ; (2) by hire ; (3) by
marriage ; the children born by any of these three
methods were equally legitimate. If a slave had
a child by her master, she was freed, and the
child was a lawful heir.

Hired wives were called *Moutaa* ; at Ispahan
the best could be hired for thirty-five pounds a
year ; when the time had expired, it could be
renewed at pleasure ; but before this was done,
the woman had to undergo forty days of purification.

Persian women, as other Easterns, wore necklaces suspended from the neck to which was
fastened a large box of sweets ; some of these
boxes were as large as the hand ; the common
ones were made of gold, the others were covered
with jewels. All were bored through and filled
with black paste, composed of musk and amber,
" but of a very strong smell."

It was common belief in this country that the
English people lived in ships on the water, and
had no possessions of land except in those of other
countries. Morier, about 1890, was of the opinion
that "Our present Persian seems still to have
retained a lingering impression of this sort."

Until a man had grown a respectable beard, he was not considered to be fit to hold any position of trust, so all young men sighed after one, and greased their chins to hasten the growth of the hairs. Yet all Persians had their head shaved ; and were never seen uncovered unless by accident.

There was in Persia a religious sect called *Gaures*, apparently an offshoot of the Christian religion especially adapted to the people. The mother of the first Prophet was called Dogdon, who, having a vision that she had been visited by an Angel, dazzling as the Sun, gave birth to the Prophet Ebrahim-zer Ateucht. This Prophet claimed that he had the power of performing miracles, and the king had him cast into prison ; but it came about that his majesty's favourite horse had his four legs cut off. Upon being consulted in regard to this tragedy, the Prophet offered up four prayers ; after each prayer the horse grew a leg, and so was wholly restored. Only half satisfied, the king tried a further test ; he made a bath of molten silver, into which the Prophet was told to bathe. This test was also satisfactory, for he came safely through this ordeal ; after this, he was said to have entered Paradise.

Then was uttered the prophecy that three more Prophets should be born ; and with the birth of the last, would come the end of the physical world ; all the mountains and metals would be precipitated into hell, fill it up and destroy it. After that all the world would be happy, each having his own mansion, their sole delight being to behold and sing praises to God and Ebrahim. This state of bliss would only, however, be the portion of those who were still alive after the " Third Coming."

There would come a day of resurrection, when the soul would re-unite with the body and appear together before the Judge of Judges; on the journey to Paradise there would be a bridge, narrower than the sharp edge of a knife, over which all Mussulmen would flit with the lightness of a bird. But the evil-doers and infidels would fall beneath this bridge into fiery furnaces, where thousands of devils armed with pincers and tridents would stir them up.

The keeper at the gate of Paradise let all good Persians enter. There, sitting in the side of a great fountain, the Prophet with a long spoon, gave them of the water to drink; after which they were presented with delicious food, and a number of women (*houris*), created expressly for this purpose, since no human woman might enter Paradise.

The *Gaures* were allowed five wives, should they be able to support them. If a man had cause to repudiate one, a year must elapse before she could be taken back; if the woman did not repent, but was willing to acknowledge her misdeed, she was given a further three years to reconsider the matter. After which time, should the pair still desire to live together again, they must be re-married, which consisted of a simple ceremony of sprinkling the face of each with water, accompanied by a few words from the priest. Although it was lawful for a man to have five wives, only one was counted as the true wife; she was compelled to share her husband's couch on Fridays and Saturdays. If after seven years she produced no children, her husband might repudiate her. By command of the prophet there was, we are told, one day in the year, in which all the women assembled to kill frogs; unfortunately,

the reason of this, and further details, are
lacking.

Both men and women *Gaures* ate pork and drank
wine ; both allowed their hair to grow, which it
did to great length ; nor did they cast aside their
nails unless the necessity arose, when they carried
away and buried the parings.

They loved bulls, cows, and dogs ; the first and
last were not allowed to be killed ; but they had
the greatest antipathy to cats, owing, they said,
to their resemblance to the devil. Thus no one
kept a cat, indeed they killed any they might find ;
should anyone have a distemper, the source was
to be found in cats who, created by the devil, had
brought about the sickness.

These people set their dead up against a walled-
in cemetery, and the flocks and crows gathered
round ; if a crow picked out the right eye of the
deceased, it was a sign of future happiness ; if
the left eye, it was a premonition of evil, and
everyone was sorrowful.

On the death of a prince, it was customary to cast
out their physicians and astrologers from court ;
firstly because they had not driven away death,
secondly because they had failed to predict it.

Another very usual custom was that when a
man was on the point of death a little dog was
placed on his chest ; when the man was *in extremis*
they applied the dog's muzzle to his mouth to
gather his soul into the dog, who would deliver
it into the hands of the Angel who is the receiver
of souls.

In *Armenia* there is a tradition that Noah
planted a vineyard near Erivan (the capital), about
two miles from the city, and that Erivan was the
most ancient inhabited place in the world.
Noah, and his family, they declared, lived there

before and after the Deluge ; and that here also was the terrestrial paradise. But Chardin says, " all this is a story . . . reported by persons equally ignorant and vain-glorious."

In the treasury of the famous monastery of the " Three Churches " there are relics of saints : an arm and thigh of St. Caiana, an arm of St. Gregory, a rib of St. James, a finger of St. Peter, and two fingers of St. John the Baptist.

Some thirty-five miles to the east of Erivan is the famous mountain in which Noah's Ark was supposed to have rested ; the Persians and Armenians called it Masis or Macis. In the Scriptures the Ark is said to have rested on the Mountain of *Ararat,* which is in Armenia. There is a tradition that the Ark is still in the Mountain of Arcis, but that no one is able to ascend the mountain to verify this statement. It is also said that in ancient days, the pitch with which the Ark was smeared was an antidote against several distempers.

We hear a quaint account of an Armenian wedding in 1831 ; the priest joined the hands of the bride and bridegroom together ; the bride was so concealed by drapery that not so much as the tip of a finger was visible, a thick white linen veil being thrown over her head. The only part uncovered was the top of her head—attached to this was a mass of false hair which frequently rested on a sofa.

At the altar the bridegroom was asked :—

" If she is blind, thou acceptest her ? "

" If she is lame, thou acceptest her ? "

" If she is hump-backed, thou acceptest her ? " To all of which questions the bridegroom replied, " I accept."

The bride was then asked :—

" Thou acceptest ? " and she replied, " I accept."

After this the bride's sumptuous clothing was removed, and her husband, for the first time, beheld his wife. For twelve months after her wedding she was not allowed to open her lips in the presence of her mother-in-law, or her married sister-in-law.

Mothers in Armenia arranged marriages without even consulting the fathers or brothers. The ceremony of affiancing was performed by a priest; children might be betrothed at the early age of two or three; even before birth, arrangements were sometimes made, subject to the arrival of the right sex. The youth was supposed to send his betrothed, every Easter, a dress; three days before the marriage was celebrated, the young man's father and mother carried to the maid's parents all the necessaries of a feast. Men and women never ate together at a public gathering; on this occasion also they ate at separate tables.

On the eve of the wedding, the bridegroom elect sent a suitably valuable dress to his betrothed while her mother sent him a costume in return. Then each, on a separate horse, was escorted by a number of young men to the church where the ceremony was performed. When night had closed in, the husband was the first to retire; his bride took off his stocking; only after the light had been extinguished, did she remove her veil. Before daybreak she arose and covered herself once again with her veil; thus, owing to this custom, there were men, who though married for ten years, had never seen the face of their wife.

We are given details, by Lady Augusta Hamilton, of another wedding. The procession was started by flute players and dancers, followed by " a group of relations "; next in the procession was a party

of men holding torches of yellow wax. Finally
the bride appeared, supported by two of her
nearest relatives ; a sack was drawn over her head
down to her feet ; a wooden " tea-board " was on
her head keeping the sack from her mouth and
nostrils ; she was separated from her bridegroom
by a party of guests. The bridegroom was a
miserable looking object, enveloped in napkins ;
his head, which was leaning slightly over his left
shoulder, was covered with a silk shawl. The
banquet which followed this lugubrious wedding
degenerated into an orgy, which lasted for three
days and nights.

In *Upper Armenia* was the famous Temple of
Fire called *Azev-beyan*, where was kept this Fire
which Fire-worshippers held to be a god. The
Guebres, the last that were left of these people,
say that the Sacred Fire is still there and can be
seen there in the shape of a flame, which, they
add, according to Chardin, " is a sort of pleasant
story, that if you make a hole in the ground, and
set a pot over it, that same fire will cause it to
seethe and boyle all that is in the pot."

On the death of a slave, before his master had
liberated him, the hand of the deceased clasped a
notice that he was honest, and his liberty was
thereby granted ; this was to clear him of the
reproach, in the next world, of being a slave.
Suicides were not carried through the door, but
through a hole in the wall.

When a high dignitary of the Church died, he
was, like an ordinary mortal, enclosed in a sack ;
but, in addition, a note was placed in his hand,
on which, quoting Tavernier, was written :
" Souvien toy que tu es venu de terre, et que
tu retourneras en terre."

PERU (ANCIENT INCAS)

It is exceedingly difficult to trace the earliest history of Peru, mixed up as it has been with contradictory accounts and untrustworthy exaggerations. Garcilasso de la Vega, the eminent Inca scholar, considers the following tradition most worthy of belief. Peru was inhabited by peoples divided up into several wild straggling tribes, continuously at war with one another, brutalized by excessive cannibalism, without law, order, or any form of morality.

It is related that an offshoot of the ancient tribe of Cocomas had a custom of eating their deceased relatives, finally grinding the bones to mix with a drink of fermented liquid—for, said they, " Is it not better to be inside a friend than be swallowed up by the black earth ? "

According to Inca Garcilasso, the people of Amtis likewise ate human flesh ; they regarded it as sacred food ; and especially relished the flesh of the sacrificed man who had died bravely and without fear, for it endowed the consumer with these desirable qualities.

Suddenly, in about the 12th century A.D., out of this chaos there arose two individuals, a man and a woman, who, under the legendary names of *Manco-Capac* and *Mama-Oello Huaco*, asserted that they were the mystical children of the Sun, destined by this heavenly father to reform and gather mankind under one Empire, and to become its rulers.

They also declared they were invested with a gold wedge, with directions that they were to journey until a spot was found where the wedge could be easily pushed into the ground. Magnetized by their splendid appearance and ancestry, and unconsciously influenced by a superior personality, the wandering tribes united and followed this remarkable pair in their mission to the valley of Cuzco. Near by, on the ridge of Huanacauti, the wedge sank into the earth at the first blow, and was never again seen.

Here, in the valley of Cuzco, were laid the foundations of the capital with its stone buildings. Under the influence of the divine wisdom of their new leaders, the tribes submitted to law and order; the spirit of these brutalized savages became changed, their vigour and energy was guided into new channels. *Manco-Capac* introduced agriculture and various industries; while *Mama-Oello* not only taught the women weaving, dyeing, spinning, etc., but presented to their minds such virtues as they had never before heard.

They were also gradually persuaded, or forced, into the belief of a Supreme Being, whom they named *Pachacamac*, and whom they credited as instilling life into the Universe. His symbol was a large oval flat plate of fine gold. All sacrifices were made with animals and birds.

Each province, town, tribe, and family retained their separate gods or totems. Every living creature was venerated for its particular physical virtue—tigers and bears for strength; monkeys for agility; dogs for fidelity; condors and eagles for their dignity. Precious stones were worshipped for their crystalline transparency and beauty of colour, the emerald being the most adored.

To those who lived by the products of the land, Earth was Mother; those living by the Sea claimed the Sea as their Mother.

There is every reason to believe that all their

laws were based on a rigorous social system ; there was no currency ; everyone, being provided with land and animals, had sufficient means to feed and clothe himself. From the earliest times their first consideration was to work the land assigned to the Sun, the product of this being stored for national purposes. Their next consideration was for the land assigned to widows, orphans, the sick or aged ; following this, the land belonging to absent soldiers was tilled during their absence ; last of all was brought under cultivation the land belonging to the Incas. There were very stringent laws pertaining to extravagance.

Thus ends the mixture of fact and fable, covering many earlier centuries of progress and culture ; and in this state they were discovered in 1516.

Thence, also, originated the powerful monarchy of the Incas, or children of the Sun. At the Assemblies of these earthly divinities, the higher orders arrived with a " light bundle," a symbol of authority, while the populace, before entering the street where the royal palace was built, were compelled to uncover their heads and remove their shoes.

According to Rivero and Tschudi, the youthful nobility, at the age of sixteen, began making preparations for a ceremony which has been compared to the order of knighthood in the Middle Ages. A grim ordeal it must have been, one at which the reigning Inca presided. Not only had the competitors to be well skilled in wrestling, and other war-like exercises, but mock tournaments were fought in which, although the weapons were without edge, the combatants were always more or less injured, and sometimes killed. Every kind of privation had also to be endured, with the dual object of rendering them fit for battle, yet making them merciful and gentle towards those who were poor and helpless. The successful competitors were then introduced to the reigning Inca, who pierced their ears with pins of gold, preparatory to the enormously heavy pendants they might afterwards be honoured with, on account of their services to the Inca. The size of the lobe of their ear was, in fact, the symbol of their status.

Some of the laws of the Peruvians were humane in the extreme : all invalids were supported at the expense of the nation. They had also special inns, the " guest houses " of those days, called *Corpahuasis*, for the assistance of strangers, which were also supported at the public expense. Another of their laws was for the purpose of instilling economy and simplicity, both in regard to food and dress. The Incas, who were also the High Priests, closely cropped their hair, obsidian knives being used for the purpose. When the Spaniards introduced scissors, razors, combs, and looking-glasses, one of the Incas is said to have remarked that the introduction of these precious articles was sufficient to give the Spaniards a claim to their country. Only the Incas wore turbans of many colours ; those of the people were of black ; to distinguish one tribe from another, the head covering was also of different shapes ; each tribe had, as well, its hair trimmed in a particular manner for the sake of distinction. There were also special rules laid down for their ear ornaments, each tribe having a decoration of its own.

The Incas always consulted the Sun and gave him as the authority, before issuing any edict, or creating a new law.

At the deathbed of the Inca, Manco-Capac, he

desired that all the people he had governed should
be known as Incas, and their wives and daughters
called Pallas.

Their punishments were particularly drastic ;
those who cheated were flogged, and occasionally
put to death ; severe sentences were also meted
out to those who removed landmarks and benefited
generally by deeds of wilful damage to their
neighbour's property. But the most brutal of all
their punishments was inflicted upon those who
seduced the women of the Incas ; such were
burnt or buried alive, with their sons, ancestors,
servants, neighbours, and cattle.

As in Greece and elsewhere, the Peruvians paid
deep respect to their dead. In October, after the
feast to their memory, they acted tragedies or
dramas, in which were commemorated the patriotic
virtues of their deceased ancestors. During the
months when their War exercises were celebrated,
they usually acted comedies, in which the warrior-
like deeds of their ancestors were recorded.

We learn from Lady Augusta Hamilton and
others that there were convents of young girls,
chosen before the age of eight, who were dedicated
to perpetual virginity as wives for the Sun. The
most celebrated was at Cusco ; here only the
daughters of the Incas of the blood royal were
admitted. They were under the charge of an
elderly dame and led a very secluded life, not
being even permitted to see their parents. Nor
might the King visit their retreat—only the Queen
and her daughters.

Other convents were so many seraglios, containing young girls of all classes famous for their
beauty ; from these were selected the Inca's
concubines. Those who were thus favoured could
not afterwards return to their convent, but became

ladies in attendance on the Queen at the Palace.
When, however, they reached mature age, they
were permitted to return to their home and
country, and in consequence of having met with
such an honour from an Inca, were much prized
as wives for the Inca's favourites, or as a reward
for men of distinction ; they were treated with
the highest respect and lived in the greatest
comfort.

An Inca might have as many concubines as he
chose, the daughters of whom were highly
honourable brides for courtiers and nobles, but
only one wife, called *Coya*, who was his sister or
half-sister : if she brought him no children, he
married all his sisters in turn. Should he have no
sisters, he espoused his next of kin : one Inca had
three hundred direct descendants. This custom
of consanguinity among the monarchs was also
common in Egypt and other oriental countries, one
convenient theory for it being that it would be
degrading to one who was considered superhuman
to mate with mere mortals ; it also assured the
ruling kingdom to the one House.

Should the Inca's wife prove unfaithful, but
swore that the Sun was the real father of her
child about to be born, she might live until she
was delivered, after which she was buried alive ;
and, according to its sex, the child of this Deity
was either destined for the priesthood, or brought
up as one of the sacred virgins.

Every year or two all the single girl connections
of the Incas, between 18 and 20, were collected
with single youths of the same status of 24—boys
not being allowed to be married before this age—
the Inca then taking the hand of each, made them
repeat a vow, after which they were considered
married. The young couple spent the honeymoon

at the home of the bridegroom's father, and became
a charge on certain districts, who were obliged to
provide for them. The following day an official
would carry out the same function with the boys
and girls of commoners, each being of similar rank
and of the same parish.

Their nearest relations in each town and district
were compelled to supply them with suitable
lodging, furniture, and means of existence.

Ordinary gentlemen might have several concubines but only one wife ; if he was unfaithful no
punishment would be inflicted were the lady
chosen a spinster ; but should she be married he
forfeited his life. When women lost their husbands
they had the choice between unsupported widow-
hood or being buried alive.

The people had a habit of washing their heads
in mud, the object being to make their hair soft
and black.

The Peruvians believed strongly in witchcraft
and considered that their downfall would arise
from these demoniacal practices ; therefore was
it commanded, that all who practised it should
be burnt, with any objects they might have used
for these unholy rites. They moreover declared
that these wizards had the power of driving some
of the highest in the land mad, by means of certain
herbs, and by forcing them to eat small stones,
who in consequence fell desperately in love with
the lower orders.

They believed, too, that the wizards had idols
of different coloured stones which they consulted ;
some of the smaller ones were in the shape of two
people embracing. When the wizards were seeking
these stones, it was declared that lightning and a
thunderbolt indicated where they would be found.
These idols were called *heracanqui*, and sold at a

high price among women, who believed they would bring them love and happiness. The idol was placed in a small new basket, with a number of blue and green feathers from special kinds of birds; amulets were also placed in the basket, as well as maize flour, some fragrant scented herbs, and cocoa leaves. It was kept among the clean clothes, the maize flour being renewed every month.

Other objects of witchcraft were also used with the same purpose, such as hairs, saliva, anything emanating from the person of the enquirer; these were mixed with some object appertaining to the person beloved. With the purpose of keeping themselves awake, wizards frequently used, after midnight, a large quantity of cocoa, green tobacco, and cinnamon. They also employed large and hairy spiders as a means of foretelling the future, seeking them in their holes, under stones in walls; having found one, the unlucky insect was either placed on the ground, or on a piece of cloth, the wizard pursuing it with a stick until its feet were broken; divination was made according to which feet were missing : even the kings consulted these magicians and followed their instructions, but only to foretell the results of war and other important national events. On entering a temple, a man would put his hand to his temple, and whether he succeeded in pulling out a hair or no, he blew in the air to the idols such as contained the evil spirit, as if blowing it a kiss.

Instead of ordinary letters, the Peruvians used two forms of writing : one, the most ancient, was a species of hieroglyphic; the other was knots made on threads of different coloured wools called *Quipos*. This is not considered to have originated in Peru, as they are heard of in Mexico and elsewhere. It was a very complicated process, with its various colours and method of intertwining as well as twisting the knots, etc. ; but it is said that the notification became so perfected that main events were recorded and interpreted : such as the list of the army, taxes, enrolment of tribes, a register of the births, deaths, etc., etc.

Architecture was one of the marvels of the Peruvians : Father Acosta speaks of a stone he measured which was 38 feet long and 18 feet wide, but says there were stones of far greater proportion. They had great fear of eclipses of the sun and moon, more especially of the latter, believing that they might explode upon the earth. To avert their ill effects, they made prodigious noises by playing upon instruments and shouting ; to add still more to the turmoil, they belaboured the dogs to make them howl. The waning of the moon they explained by declaring that the planet was sickening.

The rainbow was an object of concern ; when seen the mouth should be firmly closed and covered with the hand ; for, if opened ever so slightly, it would be the means of making the teeth rot.

Although in a much lesser degree than the Sun, the Moon as both its sister and wife, was an object of great veneration. Thunder, lightning, and thunderbolts were the Sun's executioners ; and in common with Athens and Rome, she was regarded as the protecting Deity during the period of childbirth. The Peruvians, until the arrival of the Spaniards, also worshipped, in common with the Greeks—Isis.

They believed that man consisted of two parts— the soul and the body. The one animated by an immortal spirit, the other by Earth. There was an ultimate heaven for the good as a reward for their

virtues ; a middle haven for the undistinguish-
able ; and a hell for the criminal—which was in
the centre of the Earth.

At one of their feasts they made a particular
kind of bread, into the composition of which the
blood of young children had been added. This
blood was drawn from between the eyebrows ;
the rubbing of this bread over the head, face,
stomach, arms and legs was supposed to keep
anyone immune from all sickness ; a piece of this
same substance, hanging on the outside of the
door, proclaimed that the people of that particular
house had been purified.

Every one, from the Inca downwards, was bound
to conform to this custom. After this, prayer was
offered to the Sun, begging its protection against
all that was harmful. As if in reply to this, four
extravagantly disguised couriers of the Sun, rising
out of the supposed unknown, from the four
quarters of the Earth, by touching the heads of
the Incas, acclaimed that they had been commanded to chase away all the sources of ill health.
Every one stood at their doors when these
messengers passed through the streets, at the same
time touching their own heads, faces, stomachs,
legs, and arms, etc., to make themselves immune
from disease. The same night, carrying lighted
torches, the Sun's messengers went through the
streets ridding the town from any malignant
disease ; finally the torches were thrown into the
river. The following five or six days were given
up to feasting and public rejoicings. They also
held a form of harvest thanksgiving, offering up
to the Sun a number of tame rabbits ; these were
thrown on to a fire made for the purpose.

It was customary for every man to possess two
drinking cups ; they were either of gold or silver

or even of wood, and were of exactly similar size and shape. At all the feasts there was an all-round mutual invitation to drain the cup ; the custom was for the instigator to fill both cups equally ; then holding one in each hand, if his guest was of superior rank, with compliments he was presented with the cup held in the right hand ; if inferior, he was given the one in the host's left hand. The authority for this does not state whether this custom did or did not, at the end of the day, lead to a brawl, or whether it did not usually end in a free fight.

A great feast was held every month during the year, the principal ones being always those which related to the Sun ; the most celebrated of all was held in the summer solstice. At this were assembled a vast throng of people from all the countries who were under the dominion of the Inca ; such as were unable to be present sent their sons and others of importance to represent them. The poorer classes also assembled to witness this huge throng of people, who wore their most magnificent court dresses and jewels and carried their finest arms, while servants held canopies of brightly coloured feathers and cloths above the heads of their lords as an emblem of nobility. They preferred to sacrifice twin-born animals, both because they were a rarity as well as an abnormality.

As there would not have been sufficient space in the dwellings, most of the visitors encamped in the public squares and streets. Women were sent for from the neighbouring country to prepare the food for this vast throng, and especially to knead a sort of cake composed of boiled maize. The virgins of the Sun prepared this repast for the Inca and nobles, as well as other foods which had been prepared the night before.

Previous to this feast there had been during the last three days a rigorous fast, when the only food permitted was a small portion of white raw corn and a special kind of herb. In no house was a fire allowed to be lit.

The instant the Sun's first rays fell on the neighbouring hill-top, a great shout arose from the crowd, as they burst into song and played joyous and triumphant airs on their rude instruments. The Inca then arose, and taking two golden vases filled with *chichu* (sacred liquid), prepared by the chosen virgins, he offered up the one in his right hand to the Sun by pouring it into a receptacle, from which was a tube whence it ran into the rock, thereby reaching the sacred shrine. With his left hand he poured a quantity of *chichu* into the hand of each of his family and pledged to their future prosperity.

The Inca then, with his family and the *Curacas* (conquered princes), went into the temple and offered up the two golden vases to the Sun ; the remainder of the people had to offer their gifts through the priests ; after which they all returned to the public square to assist at the sacrifices offered by the High Priest on the table or altar. Llamas were chosen for this purpose, the victim being held by four servants of the priest, with its face towards the east ; its entrails were afterwards examined to see whether the omens were propitious.

According to Inca Garcilasso, these sacrifices had been modified. The principal thank-offering to the Sun consisted of lambs, sheep and sterile animals ; also rabbits, birds and even vegetables ; including finely-made clothes, but never a human sacrifice.

Many authorities declared that human sacrifices, usually young children, were occasionally made to

the Sun; and that when young children and
youths were sacrificed, the idols buried with the
mummies lived on human flesh. It was not
unusual, especially when comets appeared or
epidemics broke out, or as an offering for mercy
for a man who was incurably ill on his deathbed, for children from the age of 4 to 10 to be
sacrificed at one time. Every year over 2000
especially prepared men were sacrificed to two
renowned gods; each part of the individual—
ears, tongue, lips and nose were solemnly offered
to the gods. Sometimes also young virgins met
with the same fate.

When an Inca or a great chief died, his wives,
concubines and servants were buried with him.
Occasionally some of the wives, who shrank from
this dreadful ordeal preferred suicide rather than
endure the life of contempt, for those who shrank
from this sacrifice, they would otherwise be
subjected to.

In the practice of medicine the Peruvians
resorted to bleeding, especially in the case of head-
aches, when they were bled from between the
eyebrows—the instrument used being a piece of
obsidian. They were well aware of the specific
values of herbs. The plant that we call tobacco
was used principally as snuff. When the Spaniards
found out its virtues they named it the " sainted
herb."

While the kings were buried in a huge sepulchre
made of stones in the form of pyramids covered
with sand, and pebbled until it resembled a small
hill, their vassals, especially in the south, were
found in gold or silver vases in the shape of urns
—their intestines having been removed—in
meadows or forests. Sometimes, also, the places
of burial had pavements and vaults. The poorer

people were often buried only a few inches below the earth, covered by a sprinkling of sand, or in such narrow fissures in the rocks that it seemed incredible how they could have been wedged in.

The ancient Peruvians were buried with their feet drawn up, their faces towards the west ; large stores of provisions in round earthen pots were also placed in the sepulchres, which were made without doors. The corpses were found muffled up in large quantities of cloth, each resembling a large statue, with a round head, two knees, and two large feet. Strong netting of coarse thread was bound over a thick mat of rushes, and in this was wrapped the corpse. When the mat was removed a large roll of cotton was seen, which entirely covered the body, and had kept two or three canes secure at the sides ; occasionally a stick was across the shoulders. Beneath this roll was another roll of red or varied coloured cloth or wool. This completely enveloped the mummy, at the end of which were one or two cloths resembling sheets ; small idols and valued stones, etc., were at the bottom of all.

The position of the mummy was " squatting," the knees drawn up to the chin, the arms either crossed over the breast or supporting the chin ; in the mouth was always a small disc of copper or gold to pay for the journey. Although in most cases the corpses were in fair preservation, the flesh had shrunk and the features were disfigured. The hair, which was black, was always in perfect preservation, but the blackness had faded and become russet coloured.

It seems never to have been proved whether this embalming was the work of man or of nature— in other words, due to the extreme dryness of the

climate ; yet it is significant that the corpses of
the Incas were in a much more perfect state of
preservation than those of the plebeian orders of
which millions have been found. In rainy districts
however, their corpses have been reduced to mere
skeletons.

The Incas had their greatest treasures buried
with them ; it was in desecrating their tombs that
their Spanish conquerors found their booty. In
the 16th century, Pope Alexander the Sixth took
upon himself to give to Portugal all the dominions
in the East ; to Spain he presented all the countries
they had discovered in the West. This donation
to his Catholic supporters embraced the whole of
the South American Continent, and included the
Empire of Peru. In 1530, a Dominican monk,
appointed for that purpose and supported by
armed soldiery, slaughtered and took prisoners the
reigning Inca of Peru, Huayna Capac, with 5000
of his unarmed and peaceful followers, for the
reason that they refused to " yeeld to the Gospell."
Thus have passed out of existence a highly civilized
people. The ethics for this wholesale slaughter by
their invaders is too obvious for comment.

PHILIPPINE ISLANDS

THE *Philippine* Islands were discovered by
Magellan in 1520, and named by the Spaniards in
honour of their king, Philip II. By the Portuguese
they were known as Manille, the ancient name
given them by Ptolemy. According to ancient
voyagers, their characteristics differed little from
those of the Malays, but the inland mountain
people had no resemblance to those on the coast.
They lived on fruit and roots, and ate monkeys,
snakes and rats. There were no universal laws ;
each tribe obeyed the patriarch of its own family.
Neither had they any specified dwelling-places—
excepting when the rains made this imperative
—sleeping in trees, on the ground, in fact wherever
darkness overtook them. The Jesuits and other
missionaries have declared that the natives had
tails, five or six inches long.

These people had a mortal dread and hatred of
the Spaniards ; if by chance they managed to kill
a solitary straggler, their delight was to drink out
of his skull. When they first saw these deadly
foes, with swords dangling from their waists,
eating hard biscuits, and puffing smoke out of
their mouths, they took them for ferocious
monsters with iron tails, eating stones, and
belching smoke.

At *Samar*, one of the islands of the group, it is
related by the natives that there was another islet
inhabited entirely by women ; this was visited
periodically by the men of an adjoining island,
who removed all male offspring of whom they
were the fathers. This islet was named the Isle
of Amazon.

Among the wild men of the hills, it was a

recognized law that anyone benefiting in any way through another became his slave. A father buying out his son from slavery immediately showed his paternal affection by making him his slave; the same compliment might be reversed, in which case the father became the slave. If a crime was committed by any individual, his whole family was held responsible and might be sold as slaves. Strangers were looked upon with suspicion—in other words as enemies. These people had a horror of theft; a liaison was merely a pastime, an exchange for a present or an excuse for giving one; for incest the culprits were put into a weighted sack and thrown into the river.

Should a man be determined to commit a murder, he first amassed as much money as possible, so as to settle with his avengers; this did not prevent his being acclaimed a brave, which carried with it the right to wear a red turban. If a man succeeded in killing seven at divers times, he could wear a turban of varied colours, called *baxache*.

Many of the natives in the island of *Suzon* were very black, with tangled hair; not tall, but remarkably strong and ferocious. They were, indeed, a great menace to their neighbours, attacking towns and often murdering the inhabitants. In the province of *Zambala* the people wore the front part of their hair shaved, and a large lock of loose hair falling over their foreheads.

In these islands the people were adepts at manufacturing poisons out of various herbs, some of which, de Morgan declares, would cause death by merely being touched by the hands and feet, or sleeping on them. There were antidotes to these poisons in other herbs, which, should they be known and found in time, would counteract their deadly effects.

In some of the provinces bows and arrows were used, but more usually lances and shields of light wood which completely covered the users. At their waste hung a dagger, four inches wide and nine inches in length ; if they encountered an antagonist, with one hand they seized hold of his hair ; with the other, with one stroke from this dagger they cut off his head, which was, later, hung up in their houses.

Lawless and savage as these people were, their first law was to honour their parents. A council of the elders settled all disputes ; in criminal cases, if the offender was unable to pay a sufficiently large recompense, his life was then and there forfeited. Payment could be made also as an atonement for murder ; but if again this was not forthcoming, the family of the deceased had the right to retaliate. In case of theft, if the thief was not known, every one who could be suspected was called upon to lay, unseen by the others, some article under a cloth spread out for the purpose —this being a hint to the thief that, if he quietly returned the missing article, no further consequences would ensue. Did this method of recovery fail, they had recourse to an ordeal. All the accused voluntarily submitted to the trial ; they plunged into a river and were totally immersed : the first one who came to the surface for breath was considered the offender ; it is hardly necessary to say that it often happened at this ordeal that many innocent people, in their attempt to prove their innocence, were drowned.

Another form of ordeal was to call upon all the suspects to snatch a stone out of a pot of boiling water ; anyone who refused was compelled to pay an equivalent value of the article stolen. Thus, apparently, in these ordeals, someone, whether innocent or guilty, would have to recompense the owner of the stolen property; and by this system all property was remarkably safely insured.

But they had the worst possible form of profiteering in nuptial fees. The bridegroom was called upon to pay when entering his house, a fee called *passava*; for speaking to his wife a toll called *patignog*; to eat and drink with her an exactment called *passalog*; finally a douceur which was called *ghinapuang*, the amount of which was in accordance to his means. These marriage levies appear to have been scooped up by the parents of his bride. In cases of infidelity, compensation was given which completely whitewashed the delinquents, removing any temporary aggravation which might have been felt; on the whole, indeed, it was considered rather a tribute to the charms of the wife.

When meeting a superior in the Philippines, the natives bent low and placed both hands on their cheeks, at the same time lifting one foot off the ground with bended knee. When meeting an equal they extended their clasped hands toward each other, bowing at the same time.

They named their newly born child from the first article, or herb, they had seen.

A man on discovering that his bride was yet a maid was deeply dissatisfied; he considered that he had chosen an unwanted—a left over, one whom no one had ever desired nor debauched. Four-footed animals were always sacrificed to their gods, and the first blow of death was given to it by a young girl.

The natives never ate alone; a man, on the loss of his wife, was served for three days during his bereavement by three widowers: a woman, on losing her husband, was looked after for the same period by three widows.

It was a custom to adopt each other in the presence of their relations. The adopted son gave over all he possessed to the one who had adopted him. In return, he was allowed to remain in his house, under his control ; and later, to receive a portion of the inheritance which came to the other sons.

Many of these people worshipped the Sun and Moon ; others held in adoration a special bird marked with yellow, which lived in the mountain woods. They had no temples nor places of public worship ; but each in his home worshipped a shrine of his own idols. Neither had they, says de Morgan, any priests, but a few old men and women, who were also reverenced as sorcerers and witches. The poor buried their dead under the floors of their houses, kept their bones for a long time in boxes and worshipped their skulls. The more wealthy used decorated coffins and placed the dead surrounded by palings, side by side with another coffin containing the deceased's most valued possessions.

POLAND

MANY centuries ago there existed a legend in Poland, which told that once there lived three brothers : their names were Lech, Czech, and Rus. These brothers met at a place since called Poynán, which was afterwards the capital of the Polish territory annexed by Germany. After a while these brothers parted, each settling in a country which was named after him. Rus gave the name to Russia, Czech to Bohemia (now Czechoslovakia), and Lech's country was called Lechia—now Poland.

One day while Lech was exploring the country, he perceived a nest of white eagles, from which is derived the Polish coat of arms ; on this spot, in course of time, a town was erected called *Gniezno*, derived from a Polish word signifying nest.

The Poles were a curiously superstitious race. In certain localities the people chased death from their villages during the spring ; this custom was associated with a variety of mystical rites, for they had a preconceived belief that winter is the season of death. Thus they connected the death of vegetation as gradually developing into death itself, and this evolved into chasing the evil which was the origin of death.

The harvest rites showed many similarities to the spring rites. The soul of a tree was either represented as a young tree, or possibly a person. The spirit, or soul, of corn was usually believed to pass into the last person who cut the sheaf—possibly the waving of the corn suggested to their minds the attempt of escape, or some birds in that sheaf conveyed the idea of the human form.

Water was regarded as a powerful factor by these people ; they believed it might even engender life. On their Easter Monday, should anyone pour water over another it was a sign of great good fortune.

On the eve of the winter solstice a special ceremony took place. The day itself was held as a fast day, but as soon as the first stars illuminated the heavens supper was served, which consisted usually only of fish, although in some districts there were as many dishes as there were apostles. The number of persons at supper must never be uneven, or it would be courting disaster. A place was always laid for a guest who had not yet arrived—maybe one from some unknown world.

These winter solstice rites are said to have been derived from a mutual origin—the feasts of Saturnalia, of the Greeks and Romans. When this feast was over the family paid a visit to the animals and the bees : when the orchard was reached the head of the family shook the fruit trees, in order to wake them, at the same time asking whether they would be fruitful. The remainder of the family then gave guarantees that the trees would bear much fruit that year.

At this season the Szopka, or Puppet Show of the Nativity, brought hence from other lands, was exhibited in the Churches ; but being considered too secular, they were afterwards taken to the churchyards, and later to the market-places and streets. On New Year's Eve a ceremony was held of chasing the Old Year. In ancient times they chased the spirits of the departed dead by cracking of whips, or in the country by beating the fences with sticks. In *Pomerania* special cakes were made which were distributed among the household, also to all the domestic animals and to male birds.

One of their customs was to fashion an effigy of death out of straw, place it on a card, and afterwards burn or drown it in the village ; this was done with the idea of exterminating death. These people had a sort of dance, when they would leap or dance with the idea of securing what each most desired : the farmer did so in order to obtain a good harvest of oats and wheat ; his wife for hemp, and the daughters for herbs.

The Poles were great believers in good and bad luck ; whether they were born in a fortunate or unfortunate moment played a very important part in the beliefs of these people. If anyone was born in an evil hour he would assuredly either die or lead a life wholly destitute of prosperity : his work, too, would he affected, such as the planting of corn ; and his purchase of cattle would be so unprofitable that he invariably sold it again to another buyer. Witches, too, those who possessed the evil eye, also unpropitious stars, all exerted their mysterious influence on such a person.

On the other hand, all that was desirable or profitable would be the portion of one who was born at a lucky moment ; it even affected such matters as borrowing (or lending). In some districts certain articles, as well as clothing, were lent up to mid-day ; in the afternoon the farmer's wife refused to lend, otherwise her feet would sorely trouble her. When persons returned what was lent or borrowed, it had to be at the same hour. In other districts milk, cheese, butter and eggs were not sold after sunset, otherwise witches would have easier access to the cows and the hens would cease laying. And should there be a baby in the hut, there must be no borrowing of anything, or prosperity would forsake the household, and the future of the infant be affected. Indeed, borrowing was prohibited for twelve days after a child was born. Should a death occur in a house, the smallest hospitality would be refused ; also the lending of mares or cows, lest it established a link between the living and the dead.

A bride must be married fasting ; and if later she became *enceinte*, mice would without doubt nibble the garments of anyone who refused her the smallest request. Among the Polish customs, when a would-be suitor arrived at the house of his beloved, before asking consent of her parents a meal might perhaps be prepared, consisting of black soup made out of duck's blood, and a water melon for dessert. Should such a meal be served, the young man knew without doubt that his suit would be rejected.

Among the superstitions was one against borrowing hot embers ; there was indeed a saying that whosoever borrowed any form of heat in this life would have to return it when he arrived in Hades. When embers were taken to a hut, one must never bid farewell to the owners, or it might cause conflagration ; but should this superstition be disregarded, the only remedy was to say, " Lift the tail of the cow."

The process of fire suggests to the primitive mind the fact of existence—the first spark ; while the extinction of fire suggests the extinction of life, in other words of death.

It was an old Polish custom that when animals were taken to market, they had to leave their stables with their heads to the door. This backward movement represented a return to their infancy, and in this way their new conditions would not harm them. Children, on the contrary, were not allowed to walk backwards, or it would have the effect of pushing their mothers into their graves.

There seems to have been a universal wish to keep some memento of an animal or fowl when it was sold, either by plucking out a small number of hairs, or a few feathers should it be a bird. In certain localities, when a farmer had purchased a horse, before taking it to its stable he tied it up in an orchard to a tree laden with much fruit, believing that by so doing it would keep in good condition. Should there, however, be no orchard, the farmer's wife would be obliged to give it its food on a cushion, so that it might grow as fat as the cushion. Even money itself was included in the superstitions of Poland, there being a strong belief that a form of witchery existed in certain of the coins.

An Inland View in Atooi.

POLYNESIA

THIS name includes a very large number of islands in the South Pacific Ocean ; the principal ones, and those best known are : Fiji, of the Fiji group ; Tonga, of the " Friendly " group ; Samoa, of the " Navigator " group ; Tahiti, of the " Society " group ; The Paumoter group ; and Easter Island.

Their existence was reported by navigators in the sixteenth century ; it was not, however, until the latter end of the eighteenth century, and especially owing to the celebrated Captain Cook's voyage in 1770, that anything definite was known of the people ; nor, except at Easter Island, have there been any records of an earlier race.

In the state in which they were discovered, there were no records beyond those handed down for about four generations ; in other words, practically from the date they first saw a white man, there seemed to have been no previous event worthy of record on which any other could be based.

From a similarity of language, features, hair, it is supposed that the inhabitants of the whole group of islands owe their origin to Malay and China, with a possible blending of Maoris from New Zealand. Most of their customs have a similarity, though in each group of islands there are rites, ceremonies, etc., which the geological formation, environment, fertility, and natural resources have evoked. For example, in the Fijis there are *men-o-bush* (bushmen) who are something infinitely wilder, more weird in their natures than the coast dwellers ; consequently some of their customs differ from those who live by fishing.

Further afield, in the Marquesas Islands, where

the land is not more than a few feet above the level of the sea, the staple food is cocoanuts and fish, which entails deep sea fishing : the inhabitants are naturally seafarers.

In islands where food is easy to procure, a state of *dolce far niente* prevails, and all rites, ceremonies, etc., are so adapted as to make the enjoyment of this state more or less complete, and in accordance with the wishes of the gods ; the desires, of course, being father to the laws of " do little," to the minimum of " don'ts." This philosophy seems also to have been the basis of their hospitality, as well as their form of communion with their gods, past and present.

Occasionally one island would raid another ; if successful they killed the male prisoners, while the females would be the spoil. This may be interpreted into Nature's law of the survival of the fittest, as well as the prevention of prolonged inter-breeding. Crime, as we know it, had no existence ; the *taboo* and their gods saw that they committed none.

TONGA ISLAND

THE consultation of the oracle in Tonga Island, of
the " Friendly " group, described by Mr. Mariner,
must have been an interesting ceremony. A hog,
yams, and other dainties having been prepared
the previous night, they were carried next morning
to the place where the priest was to be found.
The chiefs and matabooles (of next importance to
the chiefs), arrayed in mats, arrived at the same
spot. The priest then seated himself, while the
matabooles sat on each side of him forming a
semicircle. At the end was seated the man who
had prepared the *kava*, a substance derived from
chewing roots ; this was served up, according to
each man's rank, in cocoanut bowls, which have
since become of great value.

This *kava* was closely identified with many
religious ceremonies. It may be stated that no
one chewed this delectable concoction but young
persons who had clean mouths, good teeth, and
were not suffering from colds. Behind the cooks,
attendants, etc., the chiefs sat, conceiving that
such humiliation would be acceptable to the gods.

From the moment all were seated, it was
believed that the god inspired the priest, who sat
for a while with his hands clasped in front of him,
his eyes cast down. While the food was being
handed round, the matabooles occasionally consulted him. At times he replied, at others he
was apparently completely absorbed. When first
he spoke, his voice was low and much altered, but
he gradually assumed his natural voice, although
it was occasionally pitched louder. The words he
uttered were believed to be the interpretation of
the divinity who inspired him, consequently they

were spoken in the first person as though he were the god. He was usually dignified, unemotional; but occasionally he became fierce, was seized with trembling, choked with emotion, tears streamed from his eyes. Yet, both before and after this convulsion, we hear that he ate as much food as four hungry people.

When he became once more normal, he remained quiet for a time; then, taking up a club which had been purposely laid beside him, he threw it over and fixed his eyes upon it. Then looking up several times, sometimes also to the right and left of it, he finally took it up, and after a moment's pause struck the ground violently. From that moment the spirit of the god was supposed to have left the priest, who now rose and mingled with the rest of the people.

Omens were considered by the Tongas as direct communications from the gods and could be counted upon to work in agreement with their own wishes; charms were thus used to bring evil and disaster upon people by invoking the aid of these divinities, the result being usually successful; and although regarded as somewhat contemptible, they did not constitute a crime. Thunder and lightning were particularly evil omens, signifying a possible invasion, the death of a great chief, or the arrival of a European ship, etc. Should anyone happen to sneeze when setting out on an expedition, it portrayed most serious consequences. Mr. Mariner was only rescued in time from possible dire consequences, having accidentally sneezed in the king's house as he was about to perform certain rites at his father's grave.

We are given some interesting particulars of a chief's wedding. The bride was lavishly perfumed with cocoanut oil and scented with sandal-wood,

A Flatooka, or Morai in Tongataboo.

but she must have presented a somewhat grotesque appearance, for although clad in about forty yards of beautiful mats from the Navigator's Islands, which were as soft as silk, her arms stuck out from her body. Nor could she sit down owing to these encumbrances ; the only position she could adopt was a half-sitting one, leaning against her female attendants who had also to raise her when she wished to shift her position. Her principal bridesmaid, aged about five, was dressed exactly like the bride ; the others, who were several years older, wore rather fewer mats.

The party then adjourned to the *morai* (an open grass space), where the bridegroom, with many other chiefs and matabooles, was awaiting their arrival : the bride and her attendants seated themselves on the grass facing the bridegroom. Presently a woman, with her face covered with a white *gnato* (a sort of thin cotton), advanced ; she walked to the upper end, where was another woman with a large roll of *gnato*, a wooden pillow, and a bottle of oil. The veiled female took the *gnato* from the other, wrapped herself up in it, and apparently went to sleep. Directly this happened, the bridegroom took his bride by the hand, led her into the house, and seated her on his left hand.

Some twenty baked hogs were now brought into the *morai* ; an ample allowance was served out to the chiefs, each one putting it into his bosom, as it would have been *taboo* for them to touch it. The remainder of the food was scrambled for at a given signal.

The woman, who had apparently gone to sleep, now reappeared, and the bridegroom led his bride by her left hand to his house, escorted by her attendants. Everyone now having departed, he then conducted her into the house prepared for her reception, of which each of his brides had at least one, and which was covered by fencing. He then left her to have her mats removed, which were replaced by her ordinary clothing.

While she was amusing herself with talking to her women, her husband presided at a feast ; but most of the guests preferred to take their portions home, except the poorest, whose portion was so small they consumed it immediately. At this feast the bride was not present, as that would have been a serious breach of etiquette. Music and dancing now followed ; when this was ended, a kind of address on morals was delivered by one of the old matabooles.

The company having dispersed, the bridegroom went to his house and sent for his bride, who arrived immediately. Directly they had retired, the lights were extinguished ; and a man purposely placed at the door proclaimed this fact to the people by three hideous sorts of war-whoops, which he followed up by a loud and oft-repeated sound of the counch.

We are told that the word *taboo* signifies something forbidden, sacred to the gods. It was often a great preventative against stealing, or entering your neighbour's grounds, etc. All persons having once broken the *taboo* were more liable to be bitten by sharks : a complicated form of logic then arose, for anyone suspected of theft was compelled to go into water where sharks abounded ; and whoever had the misfortune to be bitten or eaten by one of these was considered to have been the thief.

Anyone touching a dead chief would be *tabooed* for ten lunar months, unless he was himself a chief, when he would be under the ban for only three, four or five, according to the rank of the dead chief. During that time he must neither feed himself, nor use a toothpick with his own hand. If there should be no one to feed him, he must go on his hands and feet, and pick up his food with his mouth. Should he disobey this, or any form of *taboo*, it was believed that he would swell up and die. To whistle was *taboo*, as it indicated a want of respect to the gods. Another example of this distressing belief was touching a chief of a higher rank, or anything which belonged to him ; before the delinquent ventured to feed himself, he must touch the feet of this higher chief, first with the palm, then with the back of each hand.

One of the curious beliefs of these people was that the liver was the seat of courage : the larger the liver, the more courageous would a man be.

Not to be tattooed was considered unmanly, so that all underwent it when they were sufficiently old ; it would also have been thought highly indecent, for although they went to battle practically naked, tattooing gave all the appearance of clothing without the encumbrance of it. Even a few women had marks on the inside of their fingers.

Unlike most of the other islands, women were usually treated with great consideration ; any other attitude would have been regarded as dastardly. A chief paid his eldest sister special respect, although this respect took the curious form of never entering the house where she was living. Among the nobility, heirs always descended in the female line.

It was a common occurrence during the illness of some great chief, that each day one of his relations should have part or the whole of their little finger cut off, to appease the gods for the ill deeds of the sick man. This operation could not have involved much pain, as Robert Kerr assures us that he has more than once seen little children quarrelling as to who should have the privilege of having their finger amputated. Children, too, were often sacrificed on the illness of their relations. Our last-named authority declares this barbarous deed was not done out of a sense of callousness and cruelty, but with the false reasoning that it was better to sacrifice one who was useless and might never grow up, on the chance that a chief whom they all revered should recover.

The funerals of great chiefs had many rites. First the body had to be washed with oil and water ; then his widows came to mourn and lament, the favourite one being strangled the following day—the day of his burial. On that day every man, woman, and child had their heads closely shaved. Several of the deceased man's most prized possessions were placed in his grave —whales' teeth, beads, valuable mats, etc. At the funeral the mourners wore old ragged mats, and leaves of the *ifi* tree. The period of mourning differed, but no man shaved his head for at least a month ; and the female mourners remained in the *fytoca* (burial-place) day and night for two months, with the exception of short visits to neighbouring houses for the purpose of eating.

The translation of the Death Lament for a fine young chief of Vavaos, wailed by his four stricken widows as they beat their breasts is typical:

> " Alas ! woe is me !
> Alas ! he is dead !
> Alas ! how I respect him !
> Alas ! how I lament his loss !
> Alas ! here are his ruins ! "

Some of the curses used by the Tongas are distinctly venomous, of which two are given : "Bake your grandfather till his skin turns to cracknell, and gnaw his skull for your share." "Dig up your father by moonlight, and make soup of his bones."

There were some unusual laws of etiquette in regard to their greatest men : when a king squatted, his attendants formed a semicircle on each side. Should the king address one of them he would reply from his seat, unless any order were given him, when he rose and seated himself in front of the king (or chief) with his legs crossed ; for rising when merely asked a question would be considered a gross act of rudeness. Even when the monarch went out for a walk, anyone he chanced to meet immediately sat down until he had passed.

These people had a custom of adopting children, even should their mothers be alive ; by this means extra necessities of life could be procured for them. Mr. Mariner had himself a foster mother who, he says, taught him many useful things : the correct pronunciation of their language, and laughing him out of any mode of dressing and customs unsuited to Tonga.*

As for their conception of a future existence, it was generally believed, that when the bodies of the higher orders died, the essence of their being became immortal. They had no ideas of future gain or punishment ; they were unable to express themselves in words, scarcely, indeed, to know what they imagined ; they had no records. Yet they were conscious of a superior power to their own, to whom all was known ; they arrived at the point of believing that each one had his own god, who would look after him so long as he did what he should do ; otherwise he would be left to misfortune and death.

Their traditions are somewhat contradictory ; one of their most ancient and widely credited was, that the gods inhabited an island called Bolotoo ; and that the Tonga Islands were drawn out of the water by the god Tangaloa, when fishing with a line and hook. Several of the minor gods were eager to visit this island, inhabited apparently, by no intelligent beings.

* When Captain Cook visited this group of islands, he had a great reception.

So about two hundred of them, male and female, started in a large canoe, and found this island so vastly to their liking, that they determined to make it their home, and broke up their canoe out of which they made smaller ones. But sickness, alas ! broke out, and several of them died. Such a catastrophe was wholly unforeseen ; moreover, one of the gods was inspired with a message from one of the gods at Bolotoo—that as they had come to this island, breathed of its air, tasted of its fruits, the decree had gone forth from the higher deities, that they must in consequence become mortal. At this they were sorely grieved, and began building other canoes. Some started, with the understanding that when they had reached the home of the Celestials, they would return for their companions ; but their companions waited in vain, for never again did they find their beloved island of Bolotoo.

RUSSIA AND TARTARY

It would be impossible to take more than a bird's-eye view of so vast a country as Russia, extending as it does on one side, from Persia almost to the Arctic Regions; on the other, from Poland to China; comprising an infinity of types, from the nomads, half barbaric tribes, to the Muscovites, with their long inheritance of savagery, their superficial coating of refinement and civilization.

Within this extensive area, existing from pre-historic days, families had expanded east and west within their characteristic latitudes; while it is probable they came into contact with other tribes, either to the north or south, probably in search of food, or for the purpose of exchange and barter. Thus there would arise a number of tribes of the same race with similar characteristics; and, centrally between them, a number of tribes of mixed races, in which existed the salient points of both. Of these last mixed people, those on the coast of the Baltic Sea, that is, between European Russia and Afghanistan, became the most powerful; their capital was Novgorod, and they were reputed to be the ancient Vandals.

At the end of their protracted war, to decide the eventual rulership—Rurick, of all the aspirants, survived; he styled himself the Lord of the whole nation, and his régime was called the Government of the Russians, the date being about 800 A.D.

For the purpose of grouping their customs, Russia includes the Western portion, the ancient home of the Goths; the Southern, Circassians and Cossacks, where it is related that the Vandals or " Wolves " originated; the Eastern, the land of the Tartars, including a number of tribes; and the Northern, the Finlanders, which also includes a number of villages reaching into the Arctic Circle.

Russia was anciently called Rosseia, meaning—a nation dispersed and scattered. One of their most marked characteristics was ultra-religious superstition. The ringing of bells was much practised, and during great festivals they were kept ringing from morn to night as an expression of adoration of the saints. Ikons or images were revered by all classes, and known by the name of *Bogh* (God) ; they were usually made in painted wood. Several villages specialized in the making of these *Boghs*, but in the negotiating of them, the word " sell " was always omitted.

In all houses these images were placed in some prominent part of the room ; when anyone entered, he immediately looked round for the ikon ; when he caught sight of it, he crossed himself and said, " Lord have mercy." He then saluted the host ; they shook hands, kissed, looked at one another, then each bowed alternately three or four times—and the greeting was over.

As an instance of the childish simplicity of the peasants—the most trivial act, such as spitting over one's shoulder, would have the desired effect on the weather. A God-fearing priest will allow himself to be dragged over a field in the hope that, touched by this magico-religious act, God will make the turnips grow round and full. Another time he might be utilized by the peasants on the land, who plucked out a few of his longest hairs by the roots, in the belief that the benevolent Creator of the Universe would, in consequence. give them an abundant harvest.

The Russians would eat neither hare nor pigeons : the former because they were " unclean," the latter—because they feared they were eating the

Saint Esprit. The number 40 was held in great veneration and, among the Jews—the sacred number of 7. St. Nicolas was their patron saint, and in 1550 the following account is given of one of his miracles : Michael Kysaletski pursued a certain renowned Tartar, and when he found he could not catch him, he said, " Oh, Saint Nicolas, bring me up with this hound." The Tartar, hearing this, cried out, " Oh, Saint Nicolas, if this man catch me by thy assistance, thou wilt perform no miracle : but if thou rescuest me, who am a stranger to this faith, from his pursuit, thy renown will be great." Report relates that Michael's horse immediately stopped, and the Tartar escaped.

In Lent, if any food were offered the poorest peasants, they would reject it with a shudder and, snatching it out of the children's hands, throw it to the dogs. During this season, the usually splendid equipages presented a wretched appearance : it is true there were several horses to each, but they were old, lame, and generally decrepit ; the harness was knotted together by broken ropes while the coachmen and footmen wore shabby, tattered liveries—all this being one of the necessary mortifications of the flesh at this particular season.

The climate of Russia is a very extraordinary one : in Moscow there is no spring : to use the words of Dr. E. D. Clarke, " Winter *vanishes*, and summer *is*." Yet the oriental habit of taking baths, and vapour baths of suffocating heat was so strong, that this practice continued even in the summer months ; and it is remarkable to read that in the public baths in winter the people would, while in a state of perspiration, roll about naked in the snow without incurring any ill effects.

Other customs the Muscovites shared in common
with the Orientals, was in ordering their slaves to
rub the soles of their feet to induce sleep ; to keep
buffoons, whose miraculous stories were to effect
the same purpose ; and in howling and tearing
their hair at the funeral of their relations.

Russian funerals were sometimes strangely
conducted : the funeral service of Prince Galitzen
was conducted with the greatest pomp, but on
the way to interment it developed into a farce.
The body was placed in an ordinary drosky,
preceded by the Prince's slaves, who were all
dressed in mourning ; and followed by the usual
poverty-stricken looking carriages used on such
occasions. We hear that the body was jolted
about in a most unseemly fashion, the priests and
the people running as fast as they were able ;
some, indeed, of the people were left straggling
behind, quite out of breath in their endeavours
to keep up with their companions.

In spite of the squalor of the peasants, which
seems to have been unparalleled, there was no
hamlet so wretched as had not its vapour bath ;
in this the whole family bathed every Saturday
and oftener during times of illness. It was quite
an ordinary sight, Joshia Conder tells us, to see
a hut with steam pouring from every chink, and
a family group—semi-nude—laughing and joking
with one another.

We are given further insight into the lives of
these peasant people by Mr. James : often, he
says, each family slept in one room, on mats or
straw, usually in their clothes. The most coveted
place was on the ledge of the stove ; infants
were packed with a few garments on to a square
canvas frame, which was hung by strings to a nail
on the wall or the ceiling.

In Moscow and St. Petersburg the accommodation for travellers is thus described : " The dirt on the floor may be removed only with an iron hoe, or a shovel. These places are entirely destitute of beds : they consist of bare walls with two or three old stuffed chairs, ragged, rickety and full of vermin." While, apparently, the condition of the walls themselves was in harmony with the rest of the room.

Noblemen might have several hundred servants yet be none the poorer, their food and clothes being obtained through the oppressed peasants ; their wages, which were rarely paid, came to about a halfpenny a day in English money. Dr Clarke says in his *Travels through Russia*, date about 1800, that the trait of extorting money and ill-treating the class just below their own was typical of the whole nation ; slaves being the lowest of all, could only vent their brutality on their wives.

The following is one of the rites regarding a Russian marriage : the bride had a crown of wormwood placed on her head as a pleasing symbol of the bitterness of wedlock. After the marriage ceremony was over, her head was sprinkled with a handful of hops by a sexton or clerk, who expressed his hope that she might prove as fruitful as that plant. She was then wrapped up in a warm coat, and conveyed by some old dames to her husband's house, a priest bearing a cross leading the way ; while one of his acolytes, who wore a rough goat skin, prayed that she might have as many children as there were hairs on his goat's skin.

When the newly wedded couple were seated at table, bread and salt were handed them, and a group of boys and girls sang the " epithalium " (nuptial benediction), which seems always to have been unnecessarily coarse ; the married pair were then escorted to their apartment by an old woman. When at last they were alone, the affectionate husband ordered his bride to pull off one of his buskins, having previously intimated that one contained a jewel or a purse of money, the other —a whip. Should the bride be so unlucky as to choose the one with the whip, it was, we hear, probable that she received a slash as a forecast of what she might expect in the future, for Russian husbands were often brutal in the extreme. It has even been said that they tortured their wives to death without punishment being inflicted. If, on the contrary, a woman, in trying to save herself from his cruelty, happened to kill him, she was buried up to her head in the ground, and died a lingering death.

The Muscovite law forbade any marital inter-course on Mondays, Wednesdays and Fridays ; should this law be disobeyed, the pair were compelled to bathe themselves before entering the church porch. Another law was held very rigidly : should a man re-marry while his wife was alive, he was forbidden to enter further into the church than the door ; if he married a third time he was excommunicated.

In 1635 Olearis gives in his *Voyage de Muscovie*, an account of how a bridegroom carried off his bride on horseback : their arrival was heralded by a rider in front, while two others armed with swords accompanied them to their house. In her triumphant progress, the bride threw pieces of cloth or red serge on the road, more especially near any ikons they happened to pass. At the marriage feast she was veiled, but was only permitted to remain a short time, when she and the bridegroom retired. At the end of two hours they returned ; and we hear that, after much eating and drinking, everyone fell asleep in one another's arms.

Polygamy was not allowed ; a widow or widower might marry, but only three times. If a bride chanced to be particularly lacking in good looks, great efforts were made that her husband should not see her until he was led up to her room. He may have had something of a shock at that moment, and we are told that men were continually cheated by a substitute.

Allowances of food in certain parts of Russia were sometimes lavish : it is stated that the labourer had an allowance of 144 lbs. of fat, and 72 lbs. of rye flour in 14 days ; while a child had 3 candles of tallow, several pounds of frozen butter, and a large piece of yellow soap. Cockrane, in his narrative of a *Pedestrian Journey*, declares that a Cossack guide consumed 20 lbs. of horseflesh a day.

The national beverage was called *quass*, made by mixing flour and water, then leaving it to ferment ; at first strangers considered it most unpalatable, its flavour resembling vinegar and water ; but after a while they found it a refreshing and delectable drink.

A custom which had died out in other countries was still prevalent in Russia in the early days of the nineteenth century : when banquets were given, all the greatest delicacies, the choicest wines, were reserved for the host and his friends, who sat at the top of the table. Those who sat at the bottom had to be content with very inferior food, and what might be left after the host and his more favoured guests had arrived at the limit of their capacity.

An amusing story is told how two English gentlemen of considerable property were travelling for pleasure in South Russia. Receiving an invitation to dinner from the " Chief Admiral," they accepted, and found themselves seated at the top of the table ; but being persistently addressed as " Milords Anglais," they declared they were no lords, merely " English Gentlemen." " Allow me then to ask," enquired their host, " what *is* the rank which you possess ? " It was then explained to these modest guests that there was no such title in Russia as " Gentleman." But, in spite of ominous silence and meaning looks, the guests obstinately declared that they had no other title than the one they had given.

The following night they returned in the most naïve way to the " Admiral's " table, and were about to resume their places of the previous evening ; but to their surprise they found each guest had moved up a place, until they, themselves, must needs be seated at the bottom of the table. In no way nonplussed, they rather congratulated themselves that they might now make a pleasant little party, further out of reach of formal etiquette.

And it is said, that in spite of dining off black bread and dirty soup, their predominating feeling was one of amusement, probably realizing the irony of the fact, that had they notified they were in His Majesty's Militia, or Members of the Volunteers in London, they might have held honoured places at the " Admiral's " banquet.

To the south of Russia, near the Baltic Sea, is the home of the *Cossack*. We are given a description of their national dance as wild and suggestive with its varied movements, particularly of the arms and head, and its short and sudden shrieks.

It has been compared to the Chinese dances, with the movements of the head from one shoulder to the other, the hands held up close to the ears.

The *Circassians*, whose country was on the border of the Black Sea, were originally Mahometans; they kept many wives, but the marriage customs of the better classes were of a far less brutal type than the Muscovites. The husband usually lived in a separate apartment of the house, and was not over fond of appearing when his wife was in the company of her friends, nor of having enquiries made in regard to her health. She was not permitted to see her parents for the first year of her marriage or until her first child was born; on this occasion her father paid her a visit, removed the cap she had worn as a maid, and threw over her the veil which would in future be her usual head-dress. For the first time he then gave her —her full marriage portion.

High-born Circassian children were removed from their parents directly after birth, and entrusted to the care of some gentleman of quality. From that time his tutor superintended the education of the sons, more particularly in all predatory adventures so common in those times; he also instructed them in the use of arms and made them a present of these, and it was in warrior's attire that they were finally introduced to their fathers.

The daughters had a poor time, being fed in a wretchedly parsimonious fashion in order to keep them slender. They were also kept constantly employed at embroidery, weaving, fashioning straw mats and baskets. Should their foster-father be so unlucky as to fail in finding a husband for them of equal birth to their own, his head was immediately cut off. Little affection existed in these aristocratic circles, more especially on the part of the fathers ; they had no wish to see their sons until they were able to bear arms, nor their daughters until they were married.

At *Karagoss*, in Tartary of the Crimea, the only part the priest took in the marriage ceremony was to visit the bride's father and ask at her window whether she was a consenting party ; in which case he said a few prayers, blessed the pair in the name of the Prophet, and withdrew. For this he received a handsome gift and either a horse, a sheep, or a present of money. The most important ceremony took place the following day, when the bride was brought to her husband's house. The bridegroom, who had previously fêted his guests, presented the most disreputable appearance as they all set out to meet the bride : he was badly dressed, ill-equipped, unshaven. As, under no circumstances, was she to be seen before entering her husband's home, her father and brother had to see to this. The carriage was draped inside with muslin, and if by mischance it arrived too early at the village, it was kept waiting at the entrance until the evening, that being the hour the inhabitants were supposed to be occupied in eating.

When the bride arrived at her new home, sherbet and a kind of sweetmeat was given her ; a lamb was also presented to her, and even put into her carriage, being afterwards removed by an attendant. Every living being having now apparently disappeared, she was wrapped in a sheet, and carried by her brother into the house, where she was placed behind a curtain in one of the private rooms. Her relations and female acquaintances then busied themselves in draping the room with gay coverings, tapestries, and cushions, etc.

In the meantime her husband, having taken farewell of most of his guests, began making his toilet, preparatory to visiting his bride : he washed, shaved, donned his most elegant dress. About midnight he was allowed to see her for about an hour, when he was summoned to withdraw. The following day he paid an early visit to his best friends, each of whom he presented with a small piece of his wife's embroidery. But custom compelled the bride to remain *standing* in the corner of the room, while receiving the guests who came out of curiosity to pay her their respects.

The primitive *Circassians* or *Kergi* were tall, the majority of them having fair hair and green eyes ; a married woman was tattooed on the nape of the neck. These people tied polished bones under their feet, and propelled themselves over the frozen snow and ice at great speed.

The *Kalmucks* inhabited the Desert between the Volga and the Don : they were nomads and worshipped idols ; moreover they had prayers attached to the end of their spears. There was little permanency in regard to their marriages for although they took but one wife, at the same time agreed to live together one year ; if there was no child when the year had expired they parted. No aspersions were cast on the woman, who was "greedily picked up for another trial." On the other hand, should a child be born, the marriage was considered lawful. No Kalmuck priest married, but he was privileged to receive hospitality from any other man's wife for one night, this being regarded by the husband as a great honour.

Among the *Tehuktchi* tobacco was the commodity most in request. Cockrane informs us that he has

seen boys and girls of 9 and 10 put a large leaf of
it into their mouths, refusing to take it out even
should meat be offered them ; in fact, " They
eat, chew, smoke and snuff tobacco all at the same
time." These people were allowed five wives, over
whom they held the power of life and death ; they
could also compel them to take " temporary "
husbands should no heir by the rightful husband
be forthcoming.

Among the *Kamschatdales*, if a man became
enamoured of a maiden, he apprenticed himself to
her father for a certain period, at the end of which
time the father either gave his consent to the
marriage, or compensated the wooer for his past
services. Should consent be given, the marriage
rites began by the would-be lover stripping his
bride of her clothing. No easy matter this, for
she was fully prepared for this emergency, being
tightly bound by girdles and closely fitting straps.
Moreover a group of women, previously selected,
were prepared to come to her assistance when
occasion demanded. And between bites and
scratches the lover was reduced to a sorry plight,
and seemed about to retire from the fray, upon
which the bride submissively entreated the return
of the bridegroom—and all was well.

Mahometan Tartars were closely veiled when
walking abroad ; should they encounter a man,
they bowed their heads and took to flight. A
story is told how an English servant, brought into
the Crimea by Admiral Mordvinof, deeming it a
monstrous act of discourtesy that women should
be forced to this expedient, whenever he met any
immediately covered his face and ran away.

This attitude on the part of a man actually
trying to avoid them, amazed these Tartar ladies
to such a pitch that they let part of their veils

slip when next they encountered him, but he ran all the faster. Their curiosity was now so inflamed that they literally "hunted" the man of misplaced chivalry, and, with veils thrown back, they pursued him to his place of retreat, where they demanded the meaning of such unaccountable behaviour.

In North Russia (Laponia) the people were expert "inchaunters"; they tied knots on a string, which hung down like a whip. When one of these was loosened "They rayse tolerable wynds"; when they loosened another "The wynd is more vehement"; and by loosening the third, "They rayse playne tempests, as in olde tyme, they were accustomed to rayse thunder and lyghtnyng." Moreover, these people were idolaters "honourying that lyvyng thyng that they meete fyrst in the mornying, for the god of that day, and dyvyning thereby theyre good luck or evyll."

They also erected great images of stone upon the mountains, which they esteemed as gods, and before which they solemnized marriages, beginning the same with fire and flint. The mystery of flint, we hear, was no less to be marvelled at in these ceremonies, for the flint "hath in it fire lying hid which does not appear until moved by force." It seems probable that these images were set up as dwelling-places for the souls of the departed great men of the tribe, thus ensuring their continued presence among their people.

This conception of ancestral reverence was carried to the highest point by a tribe on the borders of Thibet : it was a custom among these people to eat their dead parents, "so that for piety's sake they should not give their parents any other sepulchre. . . . They make handsome cups out of the heads of their parents, so that when drinking out of them they may have them in mind in the midst of their merry-making " ; perhaps, too, with the belief that the spirit of the dead was present at and taking part in the feast. It seems also possible that the ikons of later day were introduced by the priests as a substitute for family ancestors.

The Calmuck Tartars, or Tatas, were a Mongolian race, an offshoot of China. In the year 1235 these people devastated Asia and the eastern portion of Europe, including Poland, Bohemia and Hungary ; their progress was suddenly stopped by the death of the notorious Genghis, Khan of Tartary. It took a year to elect a successor : by that time they had for ever fallen out of their place as conquerors of a large portion of the world. In the beginning of the thirteenth century nearly all Christians believed them to be of the lost Tribe of Israel : the Jews of Europe, especially those of Germany, thinking the Mongols were sent by God to deliver them from the oppression of the Christians, endeavoured in 1241 to smuggle arms and provisions to them.

In appearance they have been described as being the most peculiar and repulsive-looking people, with their long greasy black hair hanging loose, broad noses, very small eyes, and enormously protruding ears. It has been further declared, " They have no religion, fear nothing, believe nothing, worship nothing but their king, who calls himself King of Kings and Lord of Lords." They have also been spoken of as a " detestable nation of Satan, inhuman and beastly, thirsting for and drinking blood, tearing and devouring the flesh of dogs and men." We are, moreover, told that they dressed in ox-hides, were devoid of laws, and that the women were taught to fight like men. In the middle of the thirteenth century they carried their tents completely set up in carts; also, that should anyone tread on the threshold of the chief, he was immediately put to death.

One of the kings, Baatu, "hath sixteene" wives; each had a separate dwelling with a number of smaller huts attached. The first wife's place in her dwelling was in the extreme West; the others were grouped near by, according to their rank, the last wife being in the extreme East. By this device the camp of a rich man resembled a small town, although the men in it were few. We are further told that " when they have erected the master's dwelling with the door to the South, his couch is set up on the North side." The side of the women was always on the East; that of the men on the West.

Over the head of the master's couch was always an image of felt like a doll, which was called the brother of the master; a similar one hung over the head of the mistress, which was called the mistress's brother. Higher up, between the two, there was " a little leane one," which represented the guardian of the dwelling. The fire was in the middle. In a conspicuous place on the right side, at the foot of the mistress's couch, was a goat's skin stuffed with wool, and near it a very small doll or puppet looking towards the attendants and women. Making the idols was a solemn ceremony; when completed a sheep was sacrificed.

The first milk of every flock and of every brood of mares was offered up to their idols, as was also the first portion of their food and drink. The heart of an animal was also offered up, left at the feet of the idol for a day, then consumed. It has been stated that some Tartars daily worshipped the animal they first saw when leaving their dwelling. Other idols, dressed like dolls, were also placed in the dwelling, while one which was kept outside, was regarded as an evil deity to be propitiated by sacrifices.

There were as many puppets in the dwelling as there were men. "They are made of straw, in which, eyes, eyebrows, and mouths are drawn ; they are dressed up to the waist. When a member of the family dies, his puppet is taken out of the house ; care is taken never to disturb nor move them." When the Tartars assembled to drink, the image over the master's head was first sprinkled, then the other images. Afterwards, with a cup they sprinkled three times to the South as a reverence to fire ; three times to the East—to air ; three times to the West—to water ; three times to the North—to the dead. This custom was common to many Mongol tribes ; the libations were usually made in the morning, before the master's first meal, which he partook of sitting on his couch, his favourite wife at his side.

They drank great quantities of the milk of mares, sheep, goats, cows or camels ; there was always some placed near the entry door ; also a musician with a reed pipe, or a kind of guitar with four, five, or nine strings. The Calmucks used also a drum, a kind of zither, a flute, and violin ; but the instrument most commonly used was a two-stringed lute.

Drunkenness was considered a fine thing among the Mongols. Carpini says, " Their food is everything that can be eaten : dogs, wolves, foxes, and even human flesh." They also eat lice, with something of the same logic as the Hottentots used, saying, " Why should I not eat them that eat my son's flesh, and drink his blood ? "

In winter they made a drink of rice mixed with honey : in summer they made one called *cosmes* or *kumiss*. This *kumiss* was the separated milk of a mare ; the butter being churned out of the pure milk the residue fermented ; it had a pungent flavour and left a taste of almonds on the tongue. " It makes the inner man most joyful, and also intoxicates weak heads " ; it may be noted that only men were allowed to milk the mares. They had also a still more alcoholic drink called *areka* which was distilled from *kumiss* ; after the butter had been separated from the milk, they dried the curd in the sun, until it was as hard as iron. This was retained for winter use, as an article of diet. Piau de Carpini says, " They do drink right shamefully and gluttonously," but we are told they were excessively careful not to drink water.

They eat all their dead animals, but only rats and mice with short tails ; the long-tailed species they refused to touch. Carpini further adds, " it is usual when one has finished eating anything out of their own separate bowls, to lick it clean, and replace it in the folds of one's gown." There was no greater sin among the Calmucks than waste ; if a guest was unwilling, or unable, to consume his share, it was customary to carry it away in his *Saptargat*, a square bag " in which they lay up their bones, when they have not time to gnaw them thoroughly " for a more leisurely meal. In this way nothing was wasted, the oldest and greatest delicacies were first exhausted, before the latest morsels were begun.

The women, who were great riders, kept pieces of horseflesh under their saddles, rendering the meat which received such a " dressing " particularly palatable to their appetites.

The coiffure in both sexes was very elaborate,

and often ornamented on the top with peacock's feathers and precious stones. The dress of the young men and maidens were so alike that it was difficult to distinguish one from the other ; their high and flat-topped hair dressing resembled a column, a rod protruded vertically through the middle : at a distance they were said to have resembled an army of soldiers with helmets.

Tartars always tied their gowns on the right side, contrary to the Turks, who always tied theirs on the left. The women we hear " are exceeding fat, and she who has the least nose is the most beautiful." They never washed clothes for fear that it might anger the gods, and produce thunder ; while wet boots, put to dry in the sun, attracted lightning.

It was customary among the Yen-ta people, that when a woman was in childbirth the husband stretched a net outside the tent and beat the air with a club until the child was born, crying the while, " Be off, devil." They had the greatest fear of thunder ; when there was a thunderstrom, they wrapped themselves up in black felt, and hid until it had passed off. Should a man be killed by lightning he was held to be a saint. It was usual for brothers to share the same wife ; should a man have no brother his wife wore a head-dress with one horn ; if, on the contrary, he had brothers, she added as many horns as there were brothers.

The Calmucks never washed the pail used for milk or curd fearing it would bring them ill luck ; as the result, the inside of their vessels had a thick coating of solidified curd, mixed with hair and dung. "When they wil wash their hands," they filled their mouths with water, and let it trickle on their hands, for according to one of their ancient laws no Mongol might put his hands in water.

When a man married he was obliged to set up a tent, and one for each of the children afterwards born ; they were of circular shape, and covered either by well fitting mats or coarse woollen cloths. A man might buy two or more sisters, but according to Vincent de Beauvais, a Tartar never considered a woman as his wife until she had borne him a child. If she proved barren he might send her away ; moreover, a husband did not obtain his wife's dowry until she had given him a son. We are also told that a man could have a hundred wives, had he the means of supporting them. They were usually selected from their own relations, with the exception of their mothers or any sisters by the same mother as himself : it was also permitted a man to marry his deceased father's widows. In the case of the death of an elder brother, it was expected that his younger brother would espouse his wife ; but she was not easily induced to re-marry, for the Calmucks believed that widows would, in a future world, return to their first husbands. If families wished to be united by marriage through young children the marriage could take place ; if the children died, the marriage contract still held good.

It was considered dishonourable for a man to pay his addresses to a girl ; her father looked round, and practically proposed to the youth of his choice, who consulted with his parents as to whether he should accept the proposal. A wooer was forbidden to enter the house of his future bride ; he had to hear from others, who knew her, all that concerned his betrothed. All marriage presents were valued by an expert, and a year later the husband sent the donors something of great value, as a return gift. In some places it would be considered immodest for her to be seen out of doors, once she was married.

Sometimes a girl went through the primitive form of marriage by riding off at full speed followed by her suitor ; if he overtook her, he made her forthwith his wife, and she returned with him to his tent. It has been stated that no girl allowed herself to be overtaken by a man for whom she had not a previous liking.

Capital punishment was carried out for a great number of offences. For horse stealing, the thief was cut in two with a sword. Among other offences, it was considered a mortal sin to leave the bit in a horse's mouth while it was feeding, but the offender was given the option of paying nine times the value of the animal. For a trivial theft, the accused was ordered to receive either 7 blows from a stick, 17, 37, or 47, etc., up to 107 blows, according to the injury received.

We are told of a wealthy and powerful Tartar who was buried in most magnificent robes, but the place of his interment was kept secret, lest his grave should be despoiled. His friends killed his horse, filling the skin with straw, which they suspended over his tomb, and having eaten the flesh, they mourned and lamented for about thirty days.

It occurred frequently that great people were buried in the following manner : a secret visit was paid into the *steppe* (plains), where a large pit was dug, and in the side of the wall of the pit a grave was made, while the slave he most dearly loved was buried under his master. When he was nearly suffocated they took him out, but this terrible ordeal was repeated three times : should he survive, he was given his freedom, and became a great man in the camp.

The dead man being now replaced in the grave, the grass was put back where it had originally grown, so that no one could find his last resting-place. Occasionally a tent was erected above the grave, in which case the body was watched and protected against all robbers. Some tribes raised tumuli over the dead, and set up a statue of the deceased, facing East, and holding a cup in its hand. Pyramids were also occasionally erected, and sometimes stone houses.

SOCIETY ISLANDS

THESE islands were named by Captain Cook in honour of the Royal Society in 1770. *Otahiti* (Tahiti) is the principal island of the group, and is said to have been discovered by Quiros at the end of the sixteenth century, all the inhabitants being usually known as Tahitians. The predominating, and probably aboriginal type is straight-haired, although, according to Captain Cook, the principal chief, Tu Vairatoa, afterwards known as Pomare, was a giant of 6 feet, 3 inches, and had a mop of hair : this being a characteristic of the Fiji Islanders, a people of different extraction.

The earliest visitors to the island record that the colour of their skin ranged from almost that of a fair European, suggesting some previous contact with white men, to that of a dark copper colour mulatto, evidence of a dark immigration. As is customary under these mixed conditions, the fairer and more rare became the dominant and aristocratic, while the darkest were the lower class. Paleness of skin was, moreover, a sign of beauty, and it was a practice among the higher orders to undergo a course of beauty culture : this consisted in remaining indoors for several months, clad in all the clothing procurable, and dieting on the bread-fruit, which was supposed to possess the remarkable quality of whitening the skin.

Whatever their various racial characteristics of colour or hair may have been, by reason of their environment they became a languorous people, irresponsible, and free of care ; occasionally, however, they tortured their prisoners to death in the most barbarous fashion.

Their dances and songs all tended in the same

THE BODY OF TEE, A CHIEF, AS PRESERVED AFTER DEATH, IN OTAHITI.

direction of exciting the amorous passions, but they held other orgies. On the occasion of going to war, they offered up a sacrifice to the god Eatooa ; Mons. de Bourgainville was an eye-witness to one of these sacrifices : after the victim was killed, probably some ne'er-do-well beach-comber (a *Toutou*), his body was trussed up to a pole by its hands and feet and laid on the beach with the feet seaward.

The chief priest then spoke to the body, and seemed to be expostulating and asking it questions, at the same time making several demands, as though the corpse could carry the message to the god, the principal wish being that the foe should be vanquished. Then followed more prayers, while hair was plucked from the corpse and made into a special " bundle." Finally a dog was killed to be served at the banquet for the god, its entrails having been first carefully examined to discover whether the omens were favourable to the expedi-tion. When the ceremony was ended, the *Toutou's* body was buried in a hole and covered with stones.

The writer before alluded to speaks of these ceremonies as religious massacres, held on frequent occasions, the object being not only to propitiate but to feed the gods. This distinctly intimates that at one time, their ancestors must have enjoyed cannibalism ; and it was the memory of these feasts of ghoulish frenzy which remained as a *bonne bouche* for the gods. It appears, also, that the left eye of the one sacrificed possessed special virtues and was reserved as food for the chief. After the battle, nearly all the prisoners were, of course, offered up to the gods. The spirits of the tribe's ancestors were supposed to be present at these feasts, both for the purpose of hearing the result of the battle, and to partake of the feast or the soul of the feast.

It may be mentioned that a writer early in the nineteenth century says in regard to human sacrifice, which prevailed from one end of the world to the other, " What then could induce mankind, universally, to imagine that sacrifices could be agreeable to a Being whom they judged superior to themselves ? " He further suggests one motive might be " some instinctive principle of our nature " or a corrupt process of the translation of tradition. It is possible to conceive it the work of some ghoul, a savage form of our " natural " or village fool, who, according to the earliest missionary, was believed to be inspired by some god ; for this reason no control was exercised over him. Although his actions were considered the deeds of the god rather than those of man, he was usually left unmolested. His life, we are told, was a lonely one of fasting and meditation ; and when the poor wretch became his own destroyer, through starvation and neglect, there were none left to lament.

From the earliest times the paramount chief relegated to himself a divine right from a celestial ancestor. He became almost too holy to touch the ground ; in Tahiti he was carried pick-a-back across the shoulders of some sturdy man : " Your king," he said, " is carried by an animal but I ride on a man," and so, by relays of strong men, he was conveyed from place to place.

Marriage was usually arranged by the parents, and when matters had been settled to their mutual satisfaction, the only remaining ceremony was to throw a piece of *tapa* (native cloth) over the bride. Her husband might discard her on any provocation, imaginary or otherwise , when men had sufficient means, they were permitted many wives.

Seeing there were no women of sufficiently high rank a chief married his sister ; since chiefs were the more able to practise polygamy, and it was an ethic of hospitality to allow other husbands, friends of the owner, the loan of their wives, it might therefore be that so-called sisters were in reality half-sisters. They even exchanged wives : there were no hard-and-fast laws in Tahiti.

A form of infanticide was practised in this island by a small body or society of extreme communists, consisting of a number of men and women, who lived promiscuously with one another. This society was known by the name of Arreoys. No outsiders were admitted to their gatherings, at which the men held wrestling bouts, while the women danced in such a manner as to excite and urge on the competitors.

If, by chance, a woman became *enceinte*, which was rare owing to the promiscuity, the child was killed at birth. Occasionally, maternal instinct asserted itself and a mother longed for her child to be spared ; the most effective way of bringing this about, was by her finding a man who was willing to adopt it ; but by this act both she and the child's father were permanently banished from the privileges and companionship of this society. The missionary, Mr. Williams, once questioned three native women in regard to the Arreoys ; one admitted that she had destroyed nine children, another seven, and another five.

The Tahitians were unable to credit the permanency of a white man's skin ; when it was exposed, they would rub it with a wetted finger. To the women especially this was a source of intense curiosity, increased also by their being covered with clothes. The first time the natives saw a man wearing boots, they exclaimed that he had iron legs.

Captain Cook's stay at Tahiti was of longer duration than that of any former navigator. He was most hospitably entertained, while the crew of his ship could hardly be restrained from accepting the candid attentions, and provocative gestures, to which they were subjected. One of the seamen was once enticed into following or chasing a woman ; not many paces from the scene he was seized, and completely stripped by a number of men, whose sole interest in the affair was to satisfy the curiosity of all the parties concerned as to the complete details of a uniform whiteness of skin : this having been ascertained, he was released and in the greatest fear rushed back to his ship.

They were a scrupulously cleanly people, bathing the whole of their body regularly three times a day in running water, however far they might be from the sea or a river. After almost each mouthful of food, they dipped their hands in water and washed out their mouths. Their covering, too, was spotlessly clean. Men and women ate at separate tables, and consumed different food ; their appetites were distinctly healthy. De la Harpe writes : "I have seen a man eat at a meal three large fish, three bread fruits each larger than two fists, fourteen or fifteen large bananas, followed by a big dish of cooked bread fruit."

To some forms of ailments, Tahitians applied friction by rubbing the muscles of the limbs with the hands, or they "kneaded" the patient much in the same manner as present-day massage. For swellings or wounds, the sufferer was placed on a pile of hot stones strewn with fresh herbs and leaves, and covered up until he was in the most profuse perspiration, when he would plunge into the sea.

Should anyone be stricken by sickness, he was considered under the ban of the gods—he had become obnoxious to them ; in other words, he was being " visited " for his sins. All the attention of his friends and relations was directed towards these divinities by offerings and addresses as well as by substantial propitiations. Whatever herbal remedies the patient might be given was not so much owing to their curative properties, but as a medium of communion with the august gods, who would answer their petitions and convey relief.

The last resort adopted for the sick man's recovery was the offer of human sacrifices, not usually from among their own tribe, but some prisoner or slave. When all efforts proved futile, the gods were first cursed, and finally dismissed, being replaced by others. If the new gods also proved a failure, the patient was left to die a lingering death from inattention and starvation. If, from the first, a case was considered hopeless, to save useless trouble, and to put him out of his misery, the sick man was usually murdered.

The king always abdicated on the birth of his firstborn son; who assumed at birth the honours of his father ; this may have been an ingenious method of avoiding any later dispute in regard to the heir. Queens as well as kings appeared in public on men's shoulders, the bearers always being deemed sacred. When chiefs who descended from the gods (those of royal blood) walked abroad, the people stripped off their upper garments as far as the waist.

There is every reason to suppose that this people had a conception of a Supreme Being called Oro ; every fabulous event, from their own origin to that of their lands, began with the metaphor 'It came to pass.' To this one god they held an evening thanksgiving for the blessing of Life. When human beings died, it was believed that their souls escaped through the nostril. They also held the belief that after a man died his body was destroyed by worms, which ultimately grew into swine ; hence hogs had souls, though of an inferior kind, and each received a distinctive name by which he was known. Some went further, and believed that even flowers and plants, preferably those used as medicinal herbs, were organized beings and possessed souls.

Every supernatural act of creation, such as rain, wind, thunder, disease, and every mysterious element in Nature, or additional superstition, resolved itself into a god. There were other malevolent gods who were ever laying traps for the unwary. It was possible to obtain the aid of one of these evil spirits by securing him to guard over your property, which meant that it became *taboo* to touch it ; this was highly effective to the owner.

In important affairs it was necessary to appeal to one particular class of gods. The needful rites and ceremonies were used to evoke that particular spirit, and cannibalism was practised as being the most potent both in regard to the properties of that particular food as well as the message foretold by the priest—as judged by the condition and position of the intestines. Pigs, dogs, and fowls were used in the same way for deciphering the message of the gods.

Apart from these primitive acts of cruelty, all voyagers have admitted that the Tahitians were a friendly disposed people. Their amusements consisted chiefly in symbolic dancing in the public spaces and wrestling matches in which both sexes

ISLAND OF OTAHITI.

took part.   Captain Bligh (who it will be remem-
bered was in command of the *Bounty*, and was
cast adrift by the mutineers on board that ship)
says, that during his visit to Tahiti the first act
of the missionaries was to destroy the wooden
idols and household gods.   When asked by some
natives, " If there is no eating, drinking, or
dancing in heaven, nor wearing of clothes, wherein
does its joyousness consist ? " the reply seems
scarcely alluring : " The joys of heaven are intel-
lectual and spiritual." The natives—evidently
preferring more material joys—begged Captain
Bligh to bring out in his next voyage a shipload
of white women.

Bankes, the scientist of Captain Cook's staff,
relates how one Sunday morning divine service was
held at the fort that had been erected on shore, to
which some Tahitian chiefs and their wives were
asked to come, for the purpose of inviting them
to ask questions on the various ceremonies.   The
chiefs followed the service intently, copying each
act of kneeling and standing, for they felt it was
a serious ceremony ; but when the service was
ended, in spite of explanations being offered, no
questions were asked.

Having witnessed this religious rite, the natives
felt that it would be only a befitting return of
courtesy to show its equivalent in their customs.
And, according to De la Harpe, they exhibited so
realistic an illustration of their marriage rites that
nothing was left to the imagination, yet without
the smallest sense of immodesty on their part.

These people were much astonished that when
the Spaniards visited them they did not bring
them presents of red feathers, as the English did
from the Friendly Islands, these being the fulfil-
ment of their greatest desires.

SOUTH AMERICAN INDIANS

THE interior and lowlands of South America were peopled by a number of aborigines, divided into numerous tribes, and sufficiently apart from one another to speak different languages. Most of the territory occupied by these Indians was a part of what is now Brazil; in various localities, their land merged into the many states round the South American coast. With the exception of a few settlements, they were mostly nomads, and varied in colour from a dark to a very pale bronze. The majority of both sexes were totally unclad. Polygamy and polyandry were universal customs among them all; and every traveller agrees that the women were usually of larger physique than the men, and that both men and women had unusually small hands and feet.

Their religion was apparently based on the same instinct as that of all primitive races, commencing with a fearsome respect for a forcible patriarchal leader; this naturally entailed a reverence both for his memory and for the rites and customs he had instituted, and was inculcated into their conscience in the form of Ancestor worship.

The Indians in these parts were originally cannibals, possibly because of the scarcity of animal food; it also being difficult to procure, owing to their not yet having mastered the use of bows and arrows. When raiding one another, only women and children under twelve were spared; the prisoners were eaten, as also those who were killed. There was an added zest to some of their feasts, in the belief that, by eating the flesh of a brave enemy chief, they absorbed his strength, and increased their own ferocity.

The *Charruas*, near La Plata river, on which stands Buenos Aires, never cut their hair, which was very long ; women wore theirs hanging down, while men tied up and decorated theirs with upstanding white feathers.

They were uncommonly verminous, and thoroughly enjoyed a feast of each other's vermin.

When a girl reached womanhood, three lines were tattooed on her face ; one from the roots of the hair on the forehead, extending to the tip of her nose ; the other two extended towards her temples. The men were ornamented by pieces of wood let into the lower lip ; neither sex ever deemed it necessary to wash their bodies or their heads ; men went about as Nature had fashioned them, never cultivated the soil, but lived upon the results of the chase.

These *Charruas* had no games, nor dances, nor songs, nor musical instruments ; they were an unemotional race, and their mien was utterly taciturn ; their nearest approach to a smile was a smirk. Neither did they raise their voice ; rather than call to anyone a few paces off, they would walk up to him and speak. So devoid of feeling were they, that they accepted death without a murmur.

At this time, the tribe had no obligatory laws, nor any chiefs in authority over them ; although, at night sentries were posted outside their huts. Should, for once, this people be stirred out of their apathy and become so human as to quarrel, they gave one another blows with their fists. When they became still more human and a man desired to set up a home, without any preliminary love-making he simply asked a girl to marry him, and we hear that he was never refused. Although polygamy was allowed no woman had more than one husband ; and brothers and sisters never married one another. Only the heads of families were permitted to indulge in the native spirit called *chicha*, which was obtained from wild honey and then allowed to ferment.

Their burial place was in some chosen hill ; the deceased man's spears and belongings were also interred with him, and should he be an adult, his nearest female relations cut off the joint of their little finger ; at each death this operation might then be repeated. De Azara says that he never saw any woman with a complete little finger. They also gave themselves deep gashes with the knife or spear of the deceased before it was entombed with him. No husband or father took any account of the death of their womenfolk.

If, however, the father of an adult man died, the son retired to his hut for two days, at the end of which time, towards night, he obtained the assistance of another man who, gripping hold of his flesh, pierced it with a pointed stick about four inches long, and there it remained like a skewer. Thus the whole of the mourner's arm was skewered up to the shoulder, and in this tortured condition he retired to the woods. With a pointed stick in his hands he contrived to dig a hole, in which he stood up all night to his chest. The following morning, he went to a hut used for the purpose, removed the skewer, and fasted for two days ; after which children and others brought him food in small quantities. This lasted for some ten or twelve days, at the end of which time he rejoined his tribe. Some pierced the flesh of their legs in a similar way, with large fish bones, as well as piercing their arms up to the elbow.

Although this self-mutilation was optional, it was very rarely omitted ; its main object being, apparently, a periodical test of endurance, which evidently did not conduce to shortening of life, for we are told that these people lived to a very old age. A shirker was regarded as a pitiable and contemptible creature.

Children remained with their parents only until they were weaned, after which they were put in charge of an uncle, cousin, or brother, and were no longer recognized by their parents. On their part, children did not mourn at the death of their father, but of their adopted father. By this custom, it would seem that all married persons brought up only adopted children.

The *Guaranys* were a race who lived on the borders of great forests ; their principal food was honey, wild fruits, and monkeys, and the inhabitants were only able to count up to four.

The natives of *Paraguay*, who were partly civilized Indians, spent most of their time from a week old, on horse-back, so it is not surprising to hear that they walked with difficulty. Since the advent of missionaries, they were so imbued with the desirability of being interred in consecrated ground, that if a man died, who lived at some distance from a church, after removing his flesh his dry bones were carried to the cemetery. Should the man live only a day's ride from the place of interment, his corpse was dressed up in his ordinary attire, he was balanced on a horse's saddle, his feet placed in the stirrups, and in this fashion he was taken to the priest.

If a man entered the church to be married, he wore his best and only clothes, but once the ceremony was performed he removed these unnecessary impediments and presented them to the priest. In ordinary conditions, should it rain, he removed what covering he wore, and placed it under shelter, for the logical reason that when the rain ceased his body would dry much quicker than the material of his clothing.

If anyone felt indisposed he would consult the first casual passer-by, and immediately sample any suggested remedy. If this remedy failed he applied to a " medicine " man, one of whom was always to be found. But the " medicine " man's only place of consultation was, on the church's feast days, on the steps of the chapel door. Nor did he see his patient, for he diagnosed the nature of the malady according to the communications made by the patient, as to whether his malady was caused by heat or cold, and prescribed accordingly.

A tribe called *Tupys*, also known as *Caribs*, acquired some fabulous notoriety ; those living in their vicinity declared that they were absolutely wild, never sleeping in the same spot on two successive nights ; that instead of talking they barked like dogs, and their lower lip was split into two divisions, for what purpose is not mentioned. When taken prisoners they made no attempt at escape, but silently—ceased to live. We further hear, that their dead were buried in a shallow grave and covered with leaves, on which were placed their bows and arrows ; while four dogs, with their feet tied, were placed at the corner of the grave. The men of the *Tupys* shaved their hair like a sort of tonsure ; and both sexes pulled out their eyebrows and eyelashes.

When the Spaniards invaded America, the women abandoned themselves with such licentious fury to the invaders, that it was a strong factor in favour of the enemy. The Spaniards on their side adopted the means, for the subjugation of the native Indians, by importing numerous

Spaniards into South America, to wed with the Indian women ; all children of these unions were considered legitimate Spanish citizens.

Guinea comprised all the territory to the north-east portion of the South American Continent, where the great rivers Orinoco and Amazon flow. The natives of these districts, though consisting of a number of different tribes, were called *Guanians* and *Caribs*. At the period of Sir Walter Raleigh's visit, in 1550, Manoa was the principal town, and also the " El Dorado " of the Spaniards. Guinea was also the home of the reputed tribe of the *Amazons*, the first authority for whose existence being Christopher Columbus. These Amazons are said to have lived on the western side of a large lake, in a country called *Woruisamoeos* ; their abode was called the " Mansion of the Sun," because " that orb sank into it." We learn also that the inhabitants cultivated their own ground, shot with bows and arrows, and used the *cura* or blow-pipe—a long tube through which poisonous darts were projected.

Sir Walter Raleigh relates that the women in the environment of Guinea " doe accompany with men but once in a yere, and for the time of one moneth, which I gather by their relation, to be in April : and that time all kings of the borders assemble, and queenes of the Amazones ; and after the queenes have chosen, the rest cast lots for their Valentines. This one moneth they feast, dance, and drinke of their wines in abundance ; and the Moone being done, they all depart to their owne provinces." Should any offspring result from this month of free love, a male infant would be returned to the father ; but the female children were kept and reared by their mothers. " If in these warres they tooke any prisoners that they used to accompany with those also at what time soever, but in the end for certeine they put them to death." Raleigh adds there are records of similar women both in Africa and in Asia.

In the Amazon country was found a kind of green stone perforated, and of cylindrical shape, which was used to cure diseases of the liver and other maladies. These stones were also used as amulets. Some Indian tribes wore these stones as a sign of chieftainship and noble lineage, their grade and nobility being recognized according to the length of the cylinder, and the depth of the perforation. A similar green stone was found in New Zealand, and used for the same purpose as the *Guanians* used them.

Sir Walter Raleigh greatly admired some of the women, and in describing the wife of a *Casique*, he says, " Shee was of good stature, with black eyes, fat of body, of an excellent countenance, her haire almost as long as her selfe, tied up againe in pretie knots. . . . I have seene a Lady in England so like to her, as but for the difference of colour, I would have sworne might have bene the same." Other writers say, that in several instances they have seen hair which touched the ground ; the women anointed it daily with oil, obtained from the Carapa nut. Among some tribes the females wore their hair short, and the men's was in long tresses or queues ; even the hair of the most aged men seldom turned white from age.

Adventurers into this land of " El Dorado " (Manoa) and Amazons, spoke of an astounding race of people, " whose heads appeare not above their shoulders " . . . they are called Ewaipan-oma : " they are reported to have their eyes in their shoulders, and their mouthes in the middle of their breasts, and that a long traine of haire

groweth backward betweene their shoulders."
The belief in this people seems to have been
common among the natives, and some English
merchants assured Raleigh that they had seen
many of them.

The *Guanians* had little use for fowls ; neither
eating their flesh nor their eggs—they regarded
them rather in the light of curiosities : but for
cocks they had a certain utility, seeing that by
their crowing they were able to judge the hours of
the night.   These people were immoderately fond
of drinking bouts. At their solemn feasts, at
which the Emperor, his governors, etc., were
present, their preparations for pledging him were
somewhat peculiar : " stripped naked, and their
bodies anointed all over with a kind of white
balsamum of which there is great plenty, and yet
very deare amongst them, and it is of all other
the most precious, whereof wee have had good
experience." When they had been thoroughly
smeared by this oil, the Emperor's servants,
"having prepared golde made into fine powder,
blow it thorow hollow canes upon their naked
bodies, untill they be all shining from the foot to
the head : and in this sort they sit drinking
by twenties, and hundreds, and continue in
drunkennesse sometimes sixe or seven dayes together."

The burying-grounds of all Indians were regarded
as very sacred ; with the dead they buried the
possessions they most valued when living. The
Orenoqueponi had apparently scant appreciation
for their spouses, for we hear they " bury not their
wives with them, but their jewels, hoping to injoy
them againe." On the other hand, the *Arwacas*
allowed their spouses to participate in the delicacies
which the corpse provided, for they " dry the

bones of their Lordes into powder, and their wives and friends drinke them in powder."

On the south side of the Orinoco, both women and children were sold to the Spaniards ; men sold their sons and daughters, or their brothers and sisters. This custom existed also among the *Guanians* and *Caribs*.

The *Waraus* were most famous boat builders, and built canoes for nearly all the colony of Demerara ; these were sometimes as long as fifty feet, and five or six feet broad, either made of cedar or a tree called Basci. These people were regarded as excessively dirty, for although their bodies were smeared with oil, they seldom troubled to wash them. They mourned their dead with great lamentations, usually burying them beneath the hut in which they had lived. Also, the chief mourner slung his hammock over the grave, and did not quit it for several days.

The *Puelches* inhabited the Southern Pampas of South America ; these people were great hunters of ostriches. The Pampas, too, was the region of large troupes of wild horses and wild cattle, which provided the inhabitants with food. Formerly, their only weapon was a sharp pointed stick, which they converted into a long spear. They also used the *bola*, which consisted of three round stones, tied together with thongs ; when thrown at a running animal, it entangled its legs, causing it to fall.

The present history of the natives of the Amazon, and Orinoco, is graphically described by Schomburgh as the finale of a tragic drama : a race of men wasting away, most of them being seized as slaves ; finally peopled by descendants of Africa, introduced into the country by the Dutch in 1621.

In this island, of which Acheen is the principal
town, the land was ploughed with buffaloes which
were very numerous, as were elephants, horses,
wild hogs, etc. Houses were raised on posts, and
built about eight feet from the ground ; they were
not luxuriant dwellings, for the roofs and walls
were covered only by mats of a very inferior quality.

When any man came into the presence of the
king, he was obliged to remove his shoes and
stockings, hold his hands above his head, and say
dowlat, after which he might sit cross-legged in his
majesty's presence. The will of the king was
paramount, and those who encountered his dis-
pleasure, might either have their hands and feet
lopped off and be banished to an island called
Pulo Wey, or suffer death by being impaled or
trodden to death by elephants.

About 1598 we are introduced to King Sultan
Aladin. He had been a fisherman in his youth,
but through his discretion and bravery, had
eventually raised himself into the position of king.
At this date he was said to be " an hundred years
old, yet is a lively man, exceedingly gross and fat."
Alas ! for King Sultan Aladin ! His years of
past discretion apparently evaporated in his old
age, for we hear that he ate and drank all day ;
" there being no end of banqueting from morning
till night " ; and when ready to burst he ate
areka betuia (*areka* being the nut, and *betel* the
leaf in which it is wrapped) ; these ingredients had
the effect of still further whetting the appetite,
and the king was able once again to return to
his banqueting. This betel nut blackened the
teeth ; hence, the blacker the teeth, the greater
admiration did the chewer evoke.

The king had three wives and a number of concubines ; his women, we are told, were his chief counsellors. His strongest force of protection on land were the elephants ; but he had also about a hundred galleys, some so large that they could carry 400 men ; these galleys were very low and narrow, open, without decks or upper works. Instead of oars, paddles about four feet long were used, made in the shape of shovels ; the king's admiral was a woman.

The religion of these people was Mahometan. They claimed to be descended from Abraham, through Ishmael, the son of Hagar. Each family or tribe had its own place of burial, which was in the fields ; they were laid to rest with their heads towards Mecca, with a curiously carved stone at the head and also at the feet. The kings, it is said, had a piece of gold at their head, and one at their feet, wondrously embossed and wrought, each weighing 500 pounds.

Once a year a singular observance was held. The king and his nobles mounted on elephants, who draped with silk and satin and cloth of gold, formed a procession to visit the Mosque, for the purpose of seeing if the *Messias* had yet arrived. The most richly adorned elephant was led ; it had a little golden castle on its back, and was intended for the use of the *Messias*. On another elephant, which had on it also a little castle, sat the king alone. Some of the mounted nobles carried golden crescents, streamers, banners, ensigns ; while drums, trumpets, and other instruments of music formed part of this gorgeous cavalcade. On arriving at the Mosque, the nobles looked into it with great solemnity ; and finding the *Messias* had not yet arrived, the king dismounted from his elephant, and rode home on the one prepared for their Prophet. The day was concluded with banqueting and games.

At a later date, about 1621, we hear the Sumatrans were great mathematicians and excelled in poetry set to music.

The people had such a reverence for their king, that in the case of lese-majesty, a brother would accuse a brother, or a son accuse his father ; on being reproached for this excess of conscience, their reply was ingenious—that God was far away, but the king was near at hand. The usual form of punishment was the bastinado. If a man accused another of seeing his wife in her bath, the culprit was sentenced to thirty strokes of a *rattan* ; but he bargained with the administrators of punishment as to the amount of the bribe, and finally walked off untouched. This satisfied both parties.

The same form of bribery was recognized in all cases. When, for instance, a man might have been sentenced to having his nose, or ears, or feet, cut off, he stipulated whether the operation should be performed by one blow, or protracted blows, such as one, two, three, or four slashes. This cruel performance was part of the king's daily entertainment. Since it was agreed that every man is frail and bound to commit some misdeed sooner or later, it was no disgrace to see men without a nose or an ear, etc.

Elephants were attached to the royal household, and they were even taught to salute his majesty ; or, when passing his palace, they bent their knees and raised their trunks three times. The king sequestered all the property of a subject who died without a male heir. Those having daughters could marry them during his life ; but if their father died before his daughters were established, they belonged to the king.

TASMANIA (VAN DIEMEN'S LAND)

TASMAN, the leader of an expedition sent by Van Diemen, the Governor of the Dutch East Indies, discovered Tasmania in 1642. The inhabitants have been described as a simple people, totally devoid of clothing except a wallaby (kangaroo skin), conveniently attached to any part of the body where most required. Their only shelter was under the bark of trees. Armed with spears, their food was anything from grubs, truffles found in the grounds, or opossums ; but after the invasions of the whites, they took every advantage of straying sheep.

It was the introduction of this diet, which practically led to their undoing ; for, to preserve the industry of sheep breeding, it was found necessary by the white population, systematically to drive into one spot the whole native population, and to confine them to one of the islands off the south-east coast of Tasmania.

As seems to have been the case with all aboriginal people, women were not taken into account at feeding time, although they cooked the food, and with the dogs shared the remnants.

The only ornaments decorating their dress was the bone, or bones, of a deceased friend, who may or may not have been stowed away in their anatomy ; cannibalism being a state of periodic necessity.

These people were ignorant of the art of boiling —everything was roasted whole just as it fell dead, whether it was wallabins, opossums, or rats ; the food was ready for eating when it burst.

The matter of sheep stealing led to much savagery on the part of both whites and blacks.

A Man of Van Diemen's Land.

Facing page 234

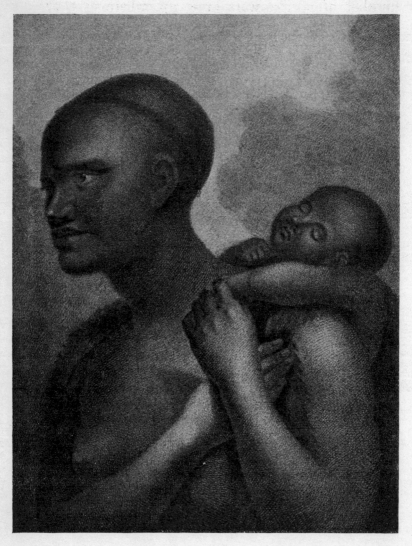

A Woman of Van Diemen's Land.

Facing page 235

To explain the law of murder to the natives, a number of notices were hung up, wherever they might be seen. These notices showed the picture of a black man spearing a white settler; accompanying it was a gallows, whereon a black man was hanging. On the same poster was a white man shooting a black, in consequence of which the white man was hanged. This form of persuasion was, however, quite ineffective.

TURKEY

THERE seems no reason to doubt that the Ottoman
Turks came originally from Turkistan, consequently they are closely allied to the Mongols.
Towards the close of the fourteenth century we
hear, according to Victor During, of their descend-
ing from the " Altai," or " Golden Mountains,"
raiding India, Persia, Syria, and Asia Minor.
Having met with repulse in 1422, they finally
succeeded in capturing Constantinople in 1453 ;
thus was laid the foundation of the great Ottoman
Empire in Europe.

The *Seraglio*, or palace of the Grand Signor,
where he kept his Court at Constantinople, consisted of a triangle about three " Italian miles "
round, at the end of the promontory Chrysorecas.
The building reached back to the top of the hill,
and from it were gardens leading down to the
sea. The Palace had high and substantial walls,
upon which were built watch towers. Some of its
many gates opened on to the sea, others into the city;
the principal gate of all opened into the city, and
was guarded by a number of white eunuchs. Inside, were black eunuchs; the chief of these was called
Kislar aga. He was a person of immense importance
and authority, both inside and outside the *harem*.

At the Seraglio, youth was trained for some of
the highest positions at Court. Here, also, at
the Harem, lived the concubines of the Grand
Signor. These consisted of a number of young
and exceedingly beautiful women, many of whom
had been sent as presents from the provinces and
the Greek islands, most of them being children of
Christian parents. After their arrival, they were
placed under the care of some old ladies, who

undertook that their charges were instructed in
music, dancing, singing, embroidery, etc. Each
had her own bed. Between every fifth slept a
governess, the principal one being called Katon
Kiâga. There being no servant, each new arrival
had to wait on the one who preceded her.

Sometimes these young girls numbered several
hundreds, according to the pleasure of the reigning
Sultan. They were never permitted to go abroad
unless he wished to travel to different places,
when black eunuchs escorted them to the boats,
which were provided with lattices and curtains.

When they journeyed by land, they travelled in
closed chariots; at various points signals were
given, so that none should approach until they
had passed. Among the Sultan's attendants was
a company of mutes, who were special adepts at
conversing rapidly by signs and gestures. There
were, also, some dwarfs for his special diversion.

Even in the garden, the little ladies were provided with a guard of black eunuchs, the premises
having been previously searched. Should anyone
have found his way into this virginal paradise,
purposely or by accident, his head was immediately cut off, and placed at the feet of the Sultan,
who presented the guard with a generous reward.
The garden, when the Sultan happened to be walking there, was the supreme opportunity of the little
ladies, to win his favour by their songs and dancing.
Lady Wortley Montagu (1717) in her visit to the
palace of the Beautiful Fatima, wife of *Kiahya-
bey*, at Adrianople, vividly and characteristically
describes the music and dancing of Fatima's
maidens : " The tunes so soft !—The motions so
languishing !—half falling back, and then recover-
ing themselves in so artful a manner, that I am
very positive, the coldest and most rigid prude

on earth could not have looked upon them without thinking of *something not to be spoke of.*"

And there were occasions when the Grand Signor permitted himself to be seduced by one of those virgin nymphs—on solemn festivals, unusual rejoicings, or the arrival of some good news.   In this case he would visit the apartment reserved for the women, and announce his choice to their governess.

The favoured nymph would then be bathed and perfumed, dressed in gorgeous apparel, and conducted by her companions, with music and singing, to the Sultan's room.   Here she would be left awhile ; then, at a given signal from the Sultan, her governess and companions returned, and escorted her back to the women's apartment, with every sign of rejoicing.   If she in the fulness of time brought forth a son, the name of *Hasseky* would be given her : and, if he became Sultan she would in addition, have a Court of her own, and a special guard of honour.

The Turkish laws forbade women to unveil to any man but the husband or relations within a certain degree. A Turk could, therefore, only judge of the looks of his future wife from the reports of his own women, or some person by whom she had been seen. A story is told, that a newly wed husband found his wife so bereft of good looks that, when two or three days later she consulted him as to which of her relations should be privileged to enter her harem, replied with resignation, " I give you my free permission, my dear, to show yourself to all the men in the world, except to myself."

In Mahomet's teachings, a man may marry a Christian or a Jewish woman, but her children must espouse the religion of his forefathers. He is prohibited from marrying an infidel. " I

withdraw my foot," says the Prophet, " and turn
away my face from a society in which the faithful
are mixed with the ungodly." Under no circumstances might a woman marry outside her own
religion. There was another matter on which
Mahomet was adamant—that the unmarried woman
died in a state of reprobation. For this reason, if
a woman preferred to remain unshackled earlier in
life, she might, when she believed death to be
approaching, try to induce some man to espouse
her.

Marriage differed from concubinage only in
regard to the dowry, which gave the wife exclusive
claim to the caresses of her husband, from
Thursday at sunset to Friday at the same hour,
which day was the Turkish Sabbath. If the
husband complied with this *family duty*, any
irregularities at other times of a Don Juan nature,
were not considered of much account.

Any child born in his house was considered
equally legitimate ; yet a husband had the right
to kill an unfaithful wife, as well as to confiscate
all her money. He might also repudiate her if she
was childless. Should her husband wish her to
return to him, before this was possible, she would
have to marry another man, and give him instant
cause to divorce her.

A wife had also a remedy for her grievances :
lack of due attention, parsimony on the part of
her husband, or her bodily fear of him. The
Chevalier d'Arvieux tells of the curious formula
she would, for this purpose, go through in the
presence of the Cadi, or Magistrate ; taking off
her shoe, and turning it upside down. Her appeal
would then be heard, and if she persisted in her
accusations she forfeited her marriage dowry, but
was free to re-marry. If, on the contrary, it was

the husband who sought a divorce, he was obliged
to give her her marriage fortune.

At the civil contract of marriage, in the time
of our Henry VIII, neither the bride nor any of her
friends were present ; but proxies, consisting of
the Cadi of the district, the priest, and a few of
her nearest relations. An important matter had
to be arranged at this contract—the settlement of
the bride's dowry, lest she became a widow or
was divorced, for in Turkey it was customary for
the bridegroom to provide the marriage portion.
Arrangements were also made at this time, in
regard to any money or land of which the bride
might be possessed. These matters having been
settled, the bridegroom's friends conveyed her
with much ceremony to her husband's house, who
undressed and put her to bed.

It was well, too, to be instructed in some matters
of etiquette ; it would, for example, have been
unpardonable for one gentleman to ask a Mahometan regarding the health of his wife. In the
same way, the Turks ridiculed uncovering the
head as a token of respect. Their mode of saluting
an equal, was to lay their hand on their heart ;
when addressing a superior, they placed their right
hand first to the mouth, then to the forehead ; if
he was a man of rank and distinction, they bent pro-
foundly, extending their right hand first towards
the ground, then raising it to their mouth and
forehead. In the presence of a sovereign, before
raising the hand to the head, they first touched
the ground. It was customary, when visiting
important inhabitants, to arrive with some offering, otherwise they would feel defrauded of a
tribute which their position demanded, and it would
be taken as somewhat of an affront ; even when
visiting inferior people one would always arrive with

a flower, an orange, or some small token of courtesy.

No Mahometan would rise to salute an infidel, whatever his position might be. A visitor of importance would be received at the foot of the stairs by two officers of the household, who supported him under the arm, until he reached the entrance of the visiting chamber, where the host advanced to welcome him. When he took his leave, the master of the house preceded him to the door of the apartment, walking a few paces in advance.

Baron de Tott had the curiosity to examine the bed laid out for him, when on a visit to a man he calls a "Dragoman." He found it consisted of fifteen mattresses of quilted cotton, each about three inches thick, covered by a sheet of Indian linen ; over this was a coverlet of green satin. There were two large pillows of crimson satin. After dinner, their amusement he tells us, consisted of swinging. He adds, " Our gentlemen with long beards took part in the frolic " ; and he continues that, " the first care of an Ottoman prince, when he comes to the throne, is to let his beard grow," this being apparently a symbol of wisdom.

But such luxuries as Baron de Tott writes of, were not commonly to be met with ; for there were no apartments in a Turkish house, says Thornton, used exclusively as bedrooms. The most usual place for sleeping was on a light mattress, which had been placed on a *sopha* in the centre of the room, or, should the temperature be sufficiently warm, in the gallery. Men and women were never fully undressed, but wore bed-gowns which, apart from their inferior quality, closely resembled the under-garments they wore in the day.

The " bed-furniture " consisted of a quilted coverlet, a sheet, and a pillow, all of which were placed in a press during the day, with which every room was provided. The *sopha* extended round three sides of the apartment, on a frame a few inches from the ground. The floor was covered by carpets or Egyptian matting, with the exception of a small part by the entrance, where the *papuches* or slippers were taken off. Chairs and tables were articles almost unknown.

Dinner was served on a large copper circular dish, placed on a low stool at the corner of the *sopha*. The guests sat round cross-legged ; the younger and less distinguished sat on cushions placed on the floor. No table-cloth was used, but a long napkin was spread over the knees of the guests. Sometimes as many as twenty or thirty dishes succeeded one another with such rapidity that it gave little chance for selection. Plates, knives and forks were dispensed with, each one helping himself with his fingers.

It was at the bagnio, or baths, that the Turkish women heard all the news and scandals of the town. To these bagnios they journeyed in their covered coaches once a week, remaining in the water some five or six hours. Their other amusements were playing chess, watching the acting of Puppet-shows, and consuming endless sweetmeats.

There was a peremptory law which forbade aliens wearing the distinctive colours of the Turks. Greeks, Armenians, and Jews, were punished for being clothed in colours forbidden to these races, and only Turks were allowed to wear yellow slippers. In regard to the Turkish citizens, laws prescribed the form of the dress, the height of the women's head-dress, and the kind of furs to be worn by each rank.

Surma was used by both men and women to beautify the eyes. It is described as " a black impalpable Powder, and so volatile as to spread itself like a fine Down upon a small brass wire, fixed in the Cork of the Bottle." The method of using it was to withdraw the Wire, without letting it touch the neck of the bottle, and to apply the extremity to the inner corner of the eye, upon which the closed eyelids rested, then drawing it gently towards the temples. This left two black streaks between the eyelids which, the Turks considered, gave an air of tenderness. They also used a kind of paint called Sulima, to whiten the skin, and to render it shiny.

As in most Oriental countries, the greatest desire of a Turkish lady was to bear children. They had, Lady Mary Montagu assures us, a special horror of seeming to have reached an age when further offspring are not to be counted upon. She frequently heard them say they hoped "*God will be so merciful as to send them two this time.*" When expostulated with by Lady M. S. Montagu on the expense of supporting so large a family, she says their reply was invariably that " the plague will certainly kill half of them."

The law did not track down a murderer, that being the duty of his nearest of kin ; not infrequently a certain payment of money, compensated the sorrowing relatives. Yet the lust of cruelty was strong among these people, for when the *Ulemats* (a class of lawyers) had offended, their goods could never be seized, nor could they be put to death, " but by being bruised in a mortar."

The Turks were great believers in amulets ; garlic was much used as a talisman. The Sultan's barge of state was preserved from harm by " a head of garlick," as was a heap of firewood in the court-yard of the public baths ; while a string of blue beads suspended round the chest of a rider, kept him safe from any malignant design

of the populace. Mothers were more inclined to
believe in the efficacy of spitting in their children's
face, to preserve it from the admiration and envy
of other women less favoured.

The Turks and Moors hung around their
children's necks the figure of an open hand, usually
the right, and also painted it upon their ships and
houses, as a charm against the " evil eye." With
them five was an unlucky number. Many of them
carried some paragraph of their Koran, which they
placed upon their breasts, or sewed under their
caps, to ward off misfortune. They even hung
these amulets round the necks of their cattle,
horses, and other beasts.

The period of mourning was regulated by law
and custom, and was a short one, mourning being
believed to be a sign of rebellion against providence.
A concession was, however, made to mothers—
that they might mourn over the death of a beloved
son for three days.

The burying-fields in Turkey were of immense
size, extending for many miles. Never was a
stone, which was at the same time a monument,
allowed to be displaced. By each stone was
erected a pillar, on the top of which was a carved
turbant, showing by their shape the profession of
the dead man. Ladies had a simple pillar devoid
of all ornament, with the exception of those who
had died unwed ; on the top of these was a rose.
Between some of these tombs was placed a chest
of ornamented stone, filled with earth ; in this were
planted herbs and aromatic flowers. They were
carefully cultivated by the females of the family,
who assembled for that purpose "in groupes."

Mingrelia, on the borders of the Black Sea, was
under the dominion of Turkey. In his *Travels*
in Turkey and Persia, in 1686, Sir John Chardin

tells us that the Mingrelians were " a People
altogether Savage. . . . They live in Wooden
Huts and go almost naked. . . . The inhabitants
makes slaves one of another, and sell one another
to the Turks and Tartars." He adds further :
" the Men are very well shap'd, and the Women
very handsome . . . with an Aspect and Proportion much to be admir'd. Besides, they have
those Obliging Glances, that win the Affections of
all that behold 'em. . . . They that are not so
handsome, or in years, paint abominably, Colour-
ing their Eyebrows, their Cheeks, Forehead, Noses
and Chins ; but the rest only paint their Eyebrows."

The same authority adds, that these people were
" Extremely Civil, full of Ceremonies and Compliments ; but otherwise the wickedest Women in
the World, Haughty, Furious, Perfidious, Deceitful,
Cruel and Impudent, So that there is no sort of
Wickedness which they will not put in Execution,
to procure Lovers, preserve their Affection, or else
to destroy 'em. . . . The Men are endu'd with all
these Mischievous Qualities with some Addition."

The Mingrelian men must have looked fearsome
beings, for we hear further that they shaved the
top of their heads in a circle, leaving the remaining
hair to grow down to their eyes, and clipping it
round at even length. " They never have but
one Shirt . . . which lasts 'em at least a Year :
in all which time they never wash 'em above
Three times : only Once or Twice a week they
shake 'em over the Fire, for the Vermin to drop off,
with which they are mightily haunted . . . which is
the reason that the Mingrelian Ladies carry a very
bad scent about 'em. I always accoasted 'em, ex-
treamly taken with their Beauty ; but I had not been
a Minute in their Company, but the Rank Whiffs from
their Skins quite stifl'd all my Amorous Thoughts."

Their sense of morality seems to have been distinctly depraved, for the same traveller relates how a certain man courted and obtained the good will of a Mingrelian Lady as his bride who, according to the custom, he would have to purchase ; but not possessing the necessary wherewithal, he planned a coup. This " coup " is thus described by our friend Chardin : " To that purpose he invited Twelve Priests to his House to hear a Solemn Mass . . . upon which the Priests went very Chearfully. . . . The Gentleman received 'em very courteously, caused 'em to say Mass, and to offer an Ox. . . . But after he had made 'em to take a Hearty Cup, he caus'd his Servants to seize 'em, Bind 'em, Shave their Heads and their Beards, and the Night following carry'd 'em to a Turkish Vessel, where he sold 'em for Household Goods, and other Necessaries, but finding he had not yet enough to pay for his Mistress, and his Nuptials, this Tyger went and fetch'd his own Wife, and sold her to the same Vessel."

The Mingrelians had not, in spite of having six bishops in their country, the smallest conception of any form of faith in their religion : their chief occupation was a continual round of feasting and banqueting and their revenue was derived from the sale of women and children into slavery to the Turks. For centuries this country had been the principal source of slaves imported into Turkey.

There being few churches with bells, the people were called together by knocking a board with a big stick. They also worshipped idols, to which they paid much reverence, clothing them with fine raiment, and decorating them with jewels. Each boasted to the idol his exploits and deeds of valour.

When a woman lost her husband, " she rends her Cloaths, strips herself naked to the Waste, tears her Hair, and with her Nails claws off the Flesh and Skin from her Body and Face . . . she crys, yells, gnashes her Teeth, foams at Mouth like a Woman mad or possess'd. . . . The men tear their Cloaths, thump their Breasts, and shave their Heads and Beards." They have, says Jean B. Tavenier (1639), a dislike to the colour blue ; they will not even touch it, because the Jews are said to have used indigo, to defile the water of Jordan.

If a married woman had several lovers, and it happened that her husband caught them unawares, he ignored them, no reference being made to the occurrence. For the more lovers a woman possessed, the more was it to her credit, being considered a proof that she was still beautiful enough to be desired—indeed it was a reproach if she had no gallants. Should the woman surprise her husband in an intrigue, she might or she might not take exception to the delicate situation. Any incompatibility of disposition was settled by the local chief, who promptly sold one or other as a slave.

The *Georgians*, who were also under the supremacy of Turkey, had a custom of building their churches upon high mountains, in remote and almost inaccessible places. These churches were not used and were allowed to fall into decay, apparently as a form of offering or atonement for their sins.

These people sometimes affianced their children when mere infants, the object being to safeguard them from becoming concubines to their lords and masters, but this we hear, " is only to be understood of those who have a larger share of decency than the generality of them."

It was customary in Georgia and Mingrelia, as in some other countries, for people before commencing a feast to go into the open, and with eyes turned towards heaven, to pour a cup of wine on the ground.

Sir John Chardin gives us several prescriptions of Georgian remedies : " For Inward Pains of what sort so ever, Take Portions of Mummy ; " " For all sorts of Falls, Bruises and Hurts Take Mummy in Drink, wrap up the Patient in a Cows Hide, and let him blood . . ." " Against a Cough, make use of the Root of the Herb call'd Hounds-Tongue or Dogs-Tongue."

THE END

AUTHORITIES QUOTED AND CONSULTED

ALVA IXTLILXOCHITL, FERNANDO DE : " Hist. Chichimèques,"
part i, pp. 266, 268, 269, 290 ; part ii, 349, 350, 353 ;
trans. H. Ternaux-Compans (1840).

ANONYMOUS : " A Late Voyage to Holland written by an
English Gentleman." London. Printed by John
Humphreys (1691).

DE AZARA, DON FELIX : tr., 1781–1801 ; pp. 9, 11, 25, 33,
71, 119, 307.

BLIGH, CAPTAIN : " A Voyage to the South Sea," pp. 97, 129.

BORWICK, JAMES, F.R.G.S. : " The Last of the Tasmanians,"
pp. 1, 5, 284–5 ; " The Daily Life of the Tasmanians "
(1870), pp. 17, 27.

BOWDITCH, CHARLES (tr. Selen) : pp. 248, 250, 251, 268, 279,
308, 347, 348, 349, 358.

BREWSTER, A. B. : " The Hill Tribes of Fiji," pp. 194, 197.

BURDER, SAMUEL : " Oriental Customs " (1808), vol. i, pp. 77,
98, 143, 202, 321–2, 345, 366 ; vol. ii, pp. 9, 47, 62, 76,
184, 228, 308, 370.

CAMPBELL, ARCHIBALD : " Voyage Round the World," 1806–
12, pp. 142, 179, 181 (1816).

CARPINI, PIAN DE : quoted from Hakluyt Soc. iii, pp. 74, 109,
112, 169, 193 (1816). Printed by Hakluyt (1598), " Texts
and Versions," pp. 109, 111, 189–90, 196.

CATLIN, GEORGE : " The North American Indians," vol. i,
pp. 6, 31, 36, 42, 51, 85, 93, 107, 126, 169, 230 (1876).

CHANTREAU : " Voyage en Russie," tr. by C., 1788–9, p. 141
(1794).

CHARDIN, SIR JOHN : " Travels," 1686 : Turkey, pp. 74, 87,
234 ; Persia, pp. 260, 263 ; Armenia, pp. 247, 504 ;
Mingrelia, pp. 76, 84.

CHURCHILL'S " Voyages IV," 1745 : (Philippines), pp. 418,
427, 428, 429, 441, quoting Gemelli-Carei. " Voyage du
Tour du Monde," tr. 1698 (Mexico), vol. i, pp. 46, 56, 58,
59, 66, 69, 121, 184, 200, 205, 212–14, 315, 317, 482, 483,
490, 491.

CLARKE, DR. E. D. : " Travels through Russia " (1800), vol. i,
pp. 46, 56, 58, 59, 66, 69, 121, 184, 200, 205, 212–14, 315,
317.

COCKRANE, JOHN DOUGLAS : "Pedestrian Journey through Russia," pp. 331, 358 (1825).

CONDER, JOSIAH : "The Modern Traveller" (1830), pp. 51, 217, 219.

COOK, CAPTAIN : Last Voyage, 1778, pp. 136–7, 296, 300, 302, 307, 314, 319, 324.

CRANTZ, DAVID : "Hist. of Greenland," tr., vol. i, pp. 149, 162, 217 (1820).

EDEN, RICHARD, 1555 : quoting Hakluyt, xii, pp. 224–5.

ELLIS, WILLIAM : "Tour through Hawaii" (1826), pp. 22, 23, 40, 407, 469 ; "Polynesian Researches" (1886), vol. i, p. 129.

FRANCKLIN, WILLIAM : "Tour from Bengal to Persia," 1786–7, quoted Pinkerton's Travels and Voyages, ix, pp. 250–1.

FRANKOWSKI, DR. EUGENJUSY (Poland).

DE GRABOWSKA, ALEXANDRA (Poland).

HAKLUYT SOC. : "Principal Navigations," x, quoting Sir Walter Raleigh.

HAKLUYT SOC., pp. 107, 111, 189, 190, 194, 196–7.
    Quoting the Journey of William de Rubruck, 1253, tr. 1903 ; and Voyage of Pian de Carpini, 1446, tr.

(18) Soc. (printed for). Tr. from Isaac de la Peyrère.
    "Hist. du Grœnland," pp. 206, 215, 225–6.

(50) Soc. (printed for). Zeno, Nicolò and Antonio.
    "Voyages to the Northern Seas in the XIV Century," p. 15.

(Ser. ii, 4) "Journey of Rubruck and Carpini," pp. 58, 144, 190, 197.

    „ VOYAGES IX, 1540.
    Quoting Fernando Alarchon, Henry Hawks, de Nica (1539), Miles Philips, p. 410, John Chilton (1568), pp. 364, 373.

    „ XII, p. 224.

HAMILTON, LADY AUGUSTA : "Marriage Rites and Customs," etc. (1822).

DE LA HARPE, iii (Congo), 190, 311, 314, 317, 345, 376, 394 ; iv (Ceylon), pp. 102, 359, 363, 371, 374, 376.

HEARNE, SAMUEL : "From Prince of Wales' Fort, Hudson Bay, to the Northern Ocean," 1769–1772 (1796), pp. 34, 121–2, 148–9, 153, 204–6, 224, 311–13, 322–36, 338, 341–3, 345–6.

HERBERSTEIN, 1550 : quoting Hakluyt, x, p. 81.

KANE, DR. : " Arctic Expedition," pp. 31, 337, 340 (1856).

KERR, ROBERT : " Travels," i (Tartary), pp. 167-9, 171-2, 174-6 ; viii (Java), 1813, pp. 55-60, 144-6 ; (Sumatra) pp. 55-58, 60 ; (Malay), pp. 190, 215 ; xvi (Society), pp. 26, 36, 144-5 (1812-13).

KOLBIN, PETER : " The Present State of the Cape of Good Hope," tr. Medley Guido, 1704, pp. 29, 46, 50, 93, 144, 158, 207, 437, 461 (1731).

LANIN, E. B. : " Russian Characteristics," pp. 88-9.

LOBO, FATHER JEROME : " Voyage to Abyssinia," trans. S. Johnson, p. 229 (1735).

MANSFIELD, PARKYNS : " Life in Abyssinia," pp. 7, 144, 207-8, 300-1.

MARINER, WILLIAM : compiled from communications of W. M., by J. Martin, 2 vols., vol. i, pp. 105-8, 133-8, 150-1, 297, 453, 456 ; vol. ii (1817), pp. 99-100, 126-8, 155-6, 225-6.

MELVILLE, HERMAN : 1814. " Four Months among the Natives of the Marquesas Islands," pp. 13, 100-2, 138, 212, 249-50.

MEROLLA : quoted Pinkerton's " Voyages," xvi (1853), pp. 229, 261, 320, 330, 345, 348.

MESSUM, CAPTAIN, C.V.S.C., R.N.

MINK, JAN, LEJEAL GUSTAVE, BOOT, G.H., and others : " La Hollande."

DE MORGA, ANTONIO, 1609 : " The Philippine Islands," tr. Hon. E. J. Stanley (1868), (Hakluyt Soc., 39), pp 282, 296, 301, 305.

NADAILLAC, MARQUIS DE : " Prehistoric America," tr. D'Anvers, pp. 31, 205, 312, 439.

OLEARIUS, ADAM : " Voyages en Muscovie, Tartarie, Perse," tr. de Wicquefort, vol. i (1769), p. 93.

PARK, MUNGO : quoted Samuel Burder.

PEACOCK, GEORGE : " Hand-book of Abyssinia," pp. 36, 43 (1867).

PEARSE, NATHANIEL : " Life and Adventures of Nathaniel Pearce by Himself," vol. ii, pp.7, 9, 26, 42 (1831).

PICART : " Religious Ceremonies," vol. iii, pp. 132, 133, 137, 187 (1731).

POTTER, JOHN, D.D. : " Archæologia Græca," 2 vols., part i, pp. 56, 145, 182 ; part ii, pp. 185, 329, 338 ; part iv, 299, 346, 375 (1813).

RALEIGH, SIR WALTER : quoted Hakluyt, x, " The Principal Navigations," pp. 361, 367, 406, 424.

RINK, DR. HENRY : " Tales and Traditions of the Esquimaux," pp. 25, 28, 36, 39, 48. " Danish Greenland," pp. 25, 117, 205 (1872).

RIVERO and TSCHUDI : " Peruvian Antiquities," tr. Francis Hawks, pp. 79, 87, 160, 185, 187, 195 (1854).

DE RUBRUCK, WILLIAM : quoted Kerr, i, " Travels." pp. 167–9, 171–2, 174–7, 231.

RUSSEL, Rev. M. : " Polynesia," pp. 94, 126, 183, 212, 216, 249, 251 (1763).

SALMON, THOMAS : " Geographical and Hist. Grammar " (1760), pp. 137–8, 430.

TAVERNIER, JEAN B., 1654–1667 : " Persian Travels," book iv, tr. Phillips, 1678, vol. i, pp. 4, 85, 163, 245, 405, 485.

THORNTON, THOMAS : " Present State of Turkey," vol. ii. (1809), pp. 107, 139, 142–3, 183–5, 221–2, 224, 234, 238–9.

DE TOTT, BARON : " Memoirs," vol. i, tr. (1786), pp. 95, 99, 125, 136, 155.

VANCOUVER, CAPTAIN GEORGE : " Voyage in the *Discovery*," vol. iii (1798), pp. 22–3, 42, 45.

DE LA VEGA, INCA GARCILASSO : " Histoire des Yucas," 2 vols., tr. J. Baudoin ; i, pp. 38, 44, 65, 79, 203, 315 ; ii, pp. 99, 139 (1867).

WALLACE, ALFRED RUSSEL : " The Malay Archipelago," vol. i (1869), pp. 271–2.

WARD, HERBERT : " A Voice from the Congo," 242–43, 245.

WILLIAMS, THOMAS : " Fiji Islands and Inhabitants," p. 287 (1824).

WILSON, REV. S. S. : " Greece, Malta, and the Ionian," p. 381 (1839).

WORTLEY MONTAGU, LADY MARY : " Letters " (1776) ; vol. ii, pp. 83, 84 ; vol. iii, pp. 11, 12, 26, 27 (1718).